We
Followed
Our Hearts
To Hollywood

By Cornelia Otis Skinner and Emily Kimbrough

OUR HEARTS WERE YOUNG AND GAY

THE LADY DESIGNER WEAKENED PERCEPTIBLY AT THIS. "YOU MEAN," SHE SAID, AND THERE WAS AWE IN HER VOICE, "THAT MISS CORNELIA OTIS SKINNER HAS A HOUSE FILLED WITH THINGS LIKE THIS HEART?"

We
Followed
Our Hearts
To Hollywood

by EMILY KIMBROUGH

DRAWINGS BY HELEN E. HOKINSON

Published by
THE BLAKISTON COMPANY, PHILADELPHIA
Distributed by

DODD, MEAD & COMPANY
NEW YORK   1943

PRINTED IN THE UNITED STATES OF AMERICA
BY AMERICAN BOOK—STRATFORD PRESS, INC., NEW YORK

To Howard Lewis with affection—
that Simon Legree of publishers,
who requested an immediate recital
of a brief trip to Hollywood

We
Followed
Our Hearts
To Hollywood

Chapter One

The three of us sat in Cornelia's office—Cornelia, her husband, Alden, and I—waiting for a telephone call. When it came Alden motioned to me in elaborate pantomime, as if we could already be heard before the telephone was taken off the hook, to listen at the other instrument. It never occurred to us to offer a receiver to Cornelia. When there is business afoot, she is likely to flutter. Also she is growing more like her mother every day and, if asked a question brusquely, will set out on a charming ramble that covers her childhood in Bryn Mawr, her married life, and every one of her thirty acres on Long Island. So while Alden and I each took a telephone, Cornelia autographed some books on her desk over in a far corner.

Hollywood was on the wire. We had been waiting for this moment for over a week. We should have been waiting for it for several months, had we not put the idea firmly out of our minds. Then when our publisher had said, "This might make a motion picture, you know," we had answered firmly, "You can't make a motion picture out of *our* book," at the same time looking at each other "with a wild surmise."

1

"Hello," Alden said in a deep, even voice. "This is Alden Blodget speaking for Miss Skinner and Miss Kimbrough." And very fortunate indeed that he was speaking for Miss Kimbrough, whose agitated voice at that moment would have covered the range of *The Star Spangled Banner*.

"Tell them," Hollywood said, "we like their book." I leered happily over at Cornelia, as if she had heard. "And ask them," Hollywood continued, "if we take it for a picture, whether they would consider coming out here to write the dialogue."

I nodded my head at Alden. He gestured at me to ask Cornelia, and went on making filling-in talk, while I covered my telephone with my hand, and hissed like a radiator, "Cornelia, listen!" She looked up from her careful penmanship. "They want us to come out to Hollywood and write the dialogue. Will you?"

"No," she said, "I can't," and went back to her autographing.

I tucked my fur coat over the telephone to shut us out from Hollywood, and hurried over to shake her by the shoulder and to demand why not. It would not take long —if we wrote fast.

She fluttered her hands, the fly leaf of our book between them, and protested, "I'm an actress. And anyway I have monologues to do, and there's Dickie. Of course Alden would be here, but Saturdays and Sundays I like to be. Of course I am not here very much anyway, but . . ."

This had all the earmarks of the beginning of a ramble. I looked across at Alden, got his eye and we both nodded. "I think they would like very much to come," Alden said.

I uncovered my telephone, hung it up, and sat down until a sudden giddiness should pass. It was all very well for Cornelia to say that she was an actress, not an author. By whatever profession she chooses to call it, she has had published several very successful books. I am certainly not an actress, and not, except for the book written with her, an author. I am a free lance writer, and this business for all its romantic Graustarkian sound, is actually like being the local seamstress, good at making things over, or running up little numbers to fill in. And why I should think that I could go to Hollywood and run up a scenario—I must have been out of my mind—I would back out— Cornelia could do it. I heard her voice, slightly hysterical in pitch, and apprehensive, "Oh Lord, Emily, you and I are going to take another trip together." And I knew that nothing would induce me to back out.

In the early 1920's we had taken a trip together to Paris, and only last year we wrote about it. We called the book *Our Hearts Were Young and Gay*. Now Hollywood was taking *Our Hearts* and asking us to follow. In all the intervening years since that trip, Cornelia and I had never traveled again together although we had remained close friends. The question was, Could our friendship survive another voyage after so long an interval? We were, un-

questionably, older now; unquestionably, too, more creatures of habit,—" 'sot' in our ways" some might have said.
But I am ever one to clap my hat on my head at the suggestion of a trip and think about it afterwards. Cornelia,
although more conservative, likes nothing better than
traveling, unless, perhaps, it is working. To have them
both offered to her in one delectable combination sand-
wich was more than her New England sense of pleasure
could resist.

"The only thing is," she said dubiously, "that when you
and I are together, Emily, THINGS happen."

I told her that was a long time ago. THINGS would
not happen to us any more. Later she was to remind me
from time to time of that pronouncement. But she finally
gave in wholeheartedly, and before I returned home to
Philadelphia the next day, we had planned every detail
of luggage and wardrobe, even to a Brownie camera and
dark glasses.

"We must have separate rooms, though," Cornelia insisted as we parted. "I'll ask for them."

I agreed. The days were gone, we knew, and not too
regretfully, when we could share, together with two dogs,
a small room in a Paris pension.

Shortly after this, Cornelia went on tour in the Middle
West. I was to join her in Chicago on the thirteenth of
February. The day before I left home, I went into town
to a luncheon given in honor of my departure. I had not

had a "going-away luncheon" in my honor since I was eleven and we went from Muncie, Indiana, to Atlantic City for the summer. Some of the children on Washington Street came over the Saturday before we left, and we had a picnic lunch in our back yard. They called it a "going-away party" and I was almost overcome by such honor. I felt the same heady exhilaration this time, which may have accounted for my buying the white satin heart for Cornelia.

She and I, in deplorable adolescence, send each other from time to time "something awful." There is a constant rivalry between us, and the pleasure of the one sending the horror greatly exceeds that of the one receiving it.

This time I saw, on Seventeenth Street, the center motif of a *gifte shoppe* window, a heart. It was about four feet high, three feet across, made of white satin, edged with, presumably, lace, about six inches wide. A wreath of red and pink roses enclosed, in the center, shining gold letters which read, "Be My Valentine." The shop owner was reluctant to sell it, but I told her that I had a friend whose tastes ran along just those lines and who might herself have designed this beautiful piece. She would certainly give it a place of honor in her house, which was really built around such things. I think I even offered to send her a picture of my friend's house with the heart in it. The lady designer weakened perceptibly at this. "You mean," she said, and there was awe in her voice, "that

Miss Cornelia Otis Skinner has a house filled with things like this heart?"

"Filled," I said firmly, "from cellar to garret." That decided her. She swept away the valentines nestled around its fringe, hoisted the giant center-piece out of the window and wrapped it up for me. Getting it out from town was quite a feat. The suburban train was crowded and highly interested. But to dispose of it on the Broadway Limited the following night was an even prettier problem. It lay on me something like a tombstone, because my berth was the only flat area large enough to support it, and it did, I think, cause some perplexity to the waiter who brought in my breakfast in the morning.

My family met me in Chicago—parents, brother and sister-in-law, a cousin and his wife—turned up unexpectedly from Muncie, with strays. My troupe met Cornelia's at the La Salle Street Station. Hers included Tante Nell. She is legitimately Cornelia's aunt, but she is by affection Tante Nell to all of Cornelia's friends who know her. Among her endearing qualities she has the live, frank curiosity of a child, and she declared now that she was not going to leave without seeing the inside of the Super Chief on which we were to travel. In a weak surprise the official let us all go through the gates—all but my brother, struggling behind and unnoticed. When he and his unwieldy package finally pushed and squeezed through, we were all together in a conspicuous group at the steps

6

of our car. A Chicago blizzard was at its peak that day. It made an ice boat of the heart, and bore my brother in a zig-zag rush of speed down the platform and through the other early passengers until he braked himself against us. Speechless, he held out the sail to Cornelia.

She said later that she was so confused by both of us having so much family and all of it there, and so astounded at my brother's flight, that it did not occur to her to wonder why he should be the messenger for such an extraordinary parcel. She presumed it must be some sort of gigantic poster display of the book which our publishers wanted us to approve, before we left. So she opened it, just as the rest of the passengers were admitted through the gate and streamed toward us. They could scarcely bear to pass her as she stood behind the heart, which was turning her, from the force of the wind, like a weather vane.

Our accommodations were a bedroom and a roomette. With a slight sense of guilt over my Valentine offering, and one look at the amount of luggage her tour had accumulated, I insisted that Cornelia take the bedroom and I would live in the roomette. We pulled out of the station waving to the long string of Kimbrough-Skinner dear ones, then ordered a drink and had dinner sent in. The promptness of its de luxe service made us begin to speculate about what Hollywood would be like. Like everything we had heard about it, I thought, only more so.

Cornelia was very serious. What was Hollywood going

to think of *us*, she wondered. After all, it knew us only through the book as naive, gauche, unworldly, always having mortifying things happen to us.

I pointed out to her that in the intervening years she had not dwelt entirely in obscurity and might be known even without the book. That cheered her a little, but she repeated somberly that even so, she supposed people would expect us to be funny. Furthermore, she said accusingly, we were not even separate individuals any more. The book had made of us something between Ruth and Naomi and—the Katzenjammer kids, she concluded bitterly.

I insisted that the incidents of the book had happened because we were young. Now we were mothers of children and respectable members of our communities, with the age for ignominious episodes far behind us. And if we were paired now, we did not have to be the Katzenjammer kids. Cornelia outlined the type she would like them to find us—dignified, charming, witty, full of grace. Her picture seemed to be a composite of Mrs. Roosevelt, Dorothy Parker, and Zorina, but I agreed that it was a fairly accurate summary of our qualities, and after this pompous exchange I left for my roomette.

It was a curious dwelling. I had never seen a roomette before and I was considerably mystified. The draped portières which separated it from the main aisle of the car seemed to me elegant but somewhat inadequate. Inside

8

WE PULLED OUT OF THE STATION WAVING TO THE LONG
STRING OF KIMBROUGH-SKINNER DEAR ONES.

the room were certain staples which I recognized, but I had heretofore found them in the sheltered privacy of a compartment, or the tenement congestion of a drawing room into which I have squeezed, for so many summers, twins and dogs with their respective paraphernalia, and myself. It was beautiful to be alone on a train, but this accommodation did seem airy, and a little Bohemian. The porter came by and showed me the bed which pulled down from the wall, and the concealed sliding door, and I was delighted to find that I was still traveling conventionally.

When I was ready for bed, however, I found that I had not listened very carefully to the porter's explanation. I remembered he had said something about pulling the bed down from the wall and fastening it somehow on the opposite side. But I am not good at taking in details and will go to almost any length rather than admit it. I was obviously, then, not going to ask the porter again to tell me how to pull down and fasten a bed.

It was apparent to me without asking anybody that I should have to hold in my arms anything I intended taking with me, because once the bed was down, there was certainly no extra room around the edges for any accessories. So I gathered up three or four books, my traveling clock, a box of kleenex in case of hay fever if it got warmer, and my hot water bottle—blistering hot. I was crowded by these articles but I kept my hands free, reached up and pulled down the bed. As I did this, my hot water bottle fell to the floor.

I know now that I should have released the bed, let it return to its niche and started again when I had retrieved the object on the floor, but I had some vague idea that if I let go, it might do something queer. So I held on firmly with my right hand and bent down to gather up my treasure in my left. Obviously, as I bent over I pulled the bed with me and at a given point in balance or gravity or something, it went ahead of its own accord and completed its task, which was to settle with a click into locks on the opposite wall. The impact of this unexpected snapping into place, coming on me as it did, stooped over and vulnerable, pushed me face down on the carpet.

My immediate problem was to get the hot water bottle out from under me as rapidly as possible. So I made as much of a Roman arch of myself as one can under a berth, and peeled the bottle off. I rested a moment then and soothed the afflicted area. After that I was concerned with getting myself out. I did not suppose that I should die; as much air, after all, would come under the bed as above it, but I was extremely uncomfortable. There would be no reason for anyone to come in and get me until Cornelia made inquiries somewhere around noon the following day, and it was now 10 P.M. It seemed a very long time to spend in any one place or position, but doubly long when the place was the Pullman carpet, and the position fine for

11

a massage, but not for fourteen hours. The porter would come if I rang but I was not able to ring. I was not able to do anything much. But I told myself sternly not to be a quitter—to think about Robert Bruce and Norman Thomas and all the other famous people who kept trying. I also squirmed, and gradually I managed to inch myself sideways over the carpet until slowly and painfully I got my arm out and up the side of the bed and my fingers reached the latch of the door. It took a long time to push it, and the strain was almost intolerable, but eventually I opened the sliding door. And I backed out into the aisle, still face down, and still holding the books, kleenex, and the traveling clock. I had to back all the way out, of course, before I could stand up, but once upright, I could move forward again, and I was in the bed, with the sliding door closed behind me in one lightning rush. I made up my mind not to mention this incident to Cornelia. But I went to sleep with an uneasy feeling that it was not the happiest omen for the composite impression she hoped we were to make.

The next day was Sunday, and as we went through the lounge car on our way to lunch, we heard a hymn being sung over the radio, and had the first inside view of our fellow passengers. The men were in pale pastel shades. The suits, I think, are called playtime clothes. The shirts, silk, were open, very wide open at the throat, disclosing chests which were densely masculine. The playtimers were almost all smoking large, black cigars, and playing gin rummy to the accompaniment of the hymns. The women were dressed exactly like the men, but they had bandannas wrapped around their heads. They all seemed to know each other.

They could not, I felt sure, be simple folk traveling for pleasure. They must be important people, all indispensable and urgently needed in Hollywood. No one on a pleasure jaunt would take accommodations on the express through which we were at the moment lurching. I had not felt before that walking a few hundred yards was one of the most perilous undertakings I had ever dared, but on this train the slightest move was an adventure, and the sense of speed like trying to catch your breath in a high wind. We rocketed past the film executives from one pastel lap to another, and through no desire on our part, came into the dining car in a skip. The head waiter stopped us and we all three moved around in what I once knew as a bunny hug, until the momentum died down. We said good morning breathily and asked for a table.

He told us, panting, that there were no tables, and would we go back to our rooms until we were called for. "You cannot stand here," he added unnecessarily.

So we retraced the whole menacing passage, eventually reaching Cornelia's room again where we sat down.

She proposed improving my geography while we waited to be called for, and I agreed. Although I try to conceal my mental inadequacies, I do not find it difficult to admit that I know nothing about geography. It is something of which one cannot pretend a knowledge without being caught—which may have something to do with my honesty. I never learned geography in school. In Muncie it was reserved for a higher grade. In Chicago, where we lived next, I was supposed to have "had" it, like mumps, which I have never had either. My father taught me, after considerable persistence, that Omaha was not a state. At college the geology professor used periodically to say on field trips, "The class may all take a rest while Miss Kimbrough endeavors to find on the map where we are," and at the end of some ten or fifteen minutes would add, coldly, "If someone will point out to Miss Kimbrough, on the map, where we are, the class will proceed."

I have always felt that it requires special talent to be able to read a map and I have also felt that it was a talent which I did not possess. Cornelia, on the other hand, is a natural map reader. She can read across a continent from right to left or from top to bottom with her hands behind her back. I have to keep the fingers of both hands in use, marking the spots I have found, while I try to locate the sea or continent I started for.

The subject of the lesson on the train was the Great Divide, and I was a humble pupil, but I think Cornelia must choose exasperating subjects to teach. In London long ago when she tried to enlighten me about British currency and wound up by saying that a guinea was a little over a pound, only there was no such thing, I slapped her; and I felt the old urge coming back. We wandered, it seemed to me, up and down and across the map in a perfectly quixotic line, and in the end it turned out to be exactly like the guinea—not really dividing anything at all.

This seemed to bring on a touch of frost in the air which we felt a drink would thaw, so we rang for the porter and ordered a cocktail for Cornelia and a beer for me. "Sorry, ladies," the porter said heartily, "we can't serve drinks in this state on Sunday. We cross the line at six o'clock this evening, and I'll be happy to serve you then."

"That's all right," Cornelia told him sweetly. "It doesn't matter a bit. Will you just bring me some ice, please?"

It did not in the least matter to her because her thoughtful husband had provided her with a bottle of Scotch for illness and other emergencies. But I, who like only beer, had another lesson in geography. It takes all day to cross the state of New Mexico, and I shall never forget it. If Sunday should happen to be the day of crossing, you cannot have a glass of beer until Arizona is reached a little after six.

And we were never called for. Instead, a waiter appeared, sent from the dining car to serve us our meals. He said it was because the dining car was so crowded that passengers were being asked to accept room service instead. But I had a conviction that it was also prompted by

15

a desire on the part of the head waiter to avoid a repetition of general dancing with us.

We read during most of the day. I had a French book which I displayed whenever I was in Cornelia's room, but back in my little roomette, I put it away immediately and brought out the detective stories with which I had come provided. Cornelia seldom reads any fiction whatever. She reads a great deal of the time, and it is invariably biography or history. This makes me a little embarrassed about my own concentration on mystery fiction, so that I displayed the French book to avoid embarrassment. Unhappily for both of us, she had it, too. I cannot imagine for what purpose she could have used this as a false front, as I was using mine, unless it were to show off to me that she had her lighter side of reading. Neither of us seemed to progress in it rapidly. We sat self-consciously, each holding the same volume, tittering from time to time as if the prose were too delicious, which it was not; but impossible to translate into English, which it was not, else I should not have been reading it.

Six o'clock came, and a bottle of beer for me, relaxation for both of us, the state of Arizona for everyone, and the realization that California was just over the next line. We were almost there. One night more on the train and in the morning we would get off at Los Angeles. Suddenly we were in a state of panic. "Do you know how to write a scenario?" Cornelia asked.

Certainly I did not, I told her, and asked when she thought *I* should ever have written one.

"I don't know," she answered, "But we ought not to have come."

Hopefully, I offered the possibility that they might not know we were there.

"We'll have to tell some one we're here when we arrive." She was somberly conscientious. "I have his name written down."

I urged her to find it. I thought that perhaps we could tell from the sound whether he would be hard to work for. Cornelia began to plunge into her bag, complaining that we did not know what hard to work for could mean. "We don't even know how to work—on a scenario. We'll have to tell him at once." I said that I shouldn't be surprised if they knew it already. They couldn't think they were hiring us for experienced scenario writers.

"Well, what are they hiring us for then?" Cornelia retorted.

I had no idea, and we were gloomily silent.

She pulled out of her bag a card and read, "Telephone Mr. D-O-Z-I-E-R—D-O-Z-E-E-A." She pronounced it with full French flavor and a baring of the teeth. I commented superfluously that he was French and that meant he would be nervous and excitable. They would speak only French, of course. I could see the whole picture. I should be lagging behind, as usual.

17

Cornelia rather brightened at that, but I went off to bed in a dark mood.

There were orange trees outside my window in the morning when I woke up, mountains in the distance with snow on the tops, and a great palm beside the water tower where we were stopping. It was unquestionably California, and by the inexorable passage of time, not far from Hollywood. I tried to think that it was exactly like the winter before when I had arrived at Los Angeles on just such a morning, bringing one of the twins for a holiday trip from her boarding school in Arizona. But considering their purposes, the two trips were no more alike than going shopping from Muncie to Indianapolis on the Interurban, and an experimental flight on a rocket ship. And I knew it.

The train started again, and I lurched my way to Cornelia's room. "Look," I said, "except for the scenery I'd rather be home."

Cornelia's back was turned to me. "If you could know," she said bitterly, "what I was thinking about you at this moment, you *would rather.*" And she wheeled around dramatically to face me, holding in front of her, like a challenge to William Tell, the white satin heart. "What can I do with this?" And she was almost tearful. "I've tried to push it down into every suitcase. The paper it was wrapped in seems to have shrunk. I certainly can*not* conceal it under my clothes, and I will not be seen with it."

In the end we folded it over and packed it in a card-

18

board dress-box; it was about as easy as folding a mattress —and we carried the box off the train ourselves. It was bulging and tied with pieces of knotted and un-matched string. We looked, as we came along the platform in the station, less like two stylish matrons from the East, than a pair of itinerant berry pickers.

As we neared the gate, I nudged Cornelia. "Photographers," I whispered happily. There they were, an eager half circle. I pulled her off to one side out of range of their vision, and we stopped to reconnoiter. I suggested that we leave the dress-box there and the other packages with it. We could come back for them later, and I asked her if I had on enough lipstick.

She told me I had and brushed a little extra powder off my chin; I altered the angle of her hat, and we re-emerged, fluttering and smiling into the camera fire. "I like this sample of your California climate," I said, idiotically, as I came up to them and paused, one foot arched in front of me like a ballerina's. Cornelia posed beside me and we looked inquiringly at the men.

One of them spoke up. "Excuse me, lady," he said, "did you happen to see Joe Louis? He's supposed to be on this train and we're here to get some shots of him."

We broke our pose abruptly and said no, we had not seen him. And we hurried on, pretending that the entire executive staff of Paramount was waiting impatiently just beyond. As it turned out, there actually was someone

19

waiting; not from Paramount, however, but from the British War Relief—a very kind Englishman named Major Glenn to whom Alden had telegraphed. Cornelia recognized him. I had never seen him before, but I joined with her in an enthusiasm which interested the photographers and surprised the major.

Our departure was a difficult maneuver, but Cornelia took charge of our escort at once, slipping her arm through his, and talking rapidly about the British War Relief, and best wishes from her husband, moving him toward the street, with a little back kick of her right foot at me. As if I did not know what had to be done! I swept with dignity back through another gate toward the train again, and furtively retrieved the cardboard dress-box and other parcels. The major was tall, good looking, very clipped as to mustache and accent, and he thought the packages were mine. I could see from the gleam in Cornelia's eye that she was having her retaliation for the satin heart, but it was hard to bear. He came from the car across the sidewalk to meet me, and stowed the packages in the luggage compartment, but he also stowed me firmly in the back seat and talked to her all the way to the hotel.

The hotel was a large French château, set in a grove of dark eucalyptus trees. Waiting for the bellboys, we stood a moment on the sidewalk, looking up at its elaborate gray stone towers, while the major patted Cornelia's hand and asked if there were anything further he might do for her.

ONE OF THEM SPOKE UP. "EXCUSE ME, LADY," HE SAID, "DID YOU HAPPEN TO SEE JOE LOUIS? HE'S SUPPOSED TO BE ON THIS TRAIN AND WE'RE HERE TO GET SOME SHOTS OF HIM."

He said over his shoulder, when they came, "Miss Kimbrough has some packages in the luggage compartment."

Miss Kimbrough stamped away into the hotel behind the boys and the cardboard box, and when Cornelia joined me, I was at the desk talking to the clerk. I told her that the clerk said our accommodations were ready and I hoped he understood that we wanted them separate.

"If we can't each have a sitting room, you take it," Cornelia murmured in the elevator. "You were in the roomette on the train."

We were still wrangling politely when the clerk opened a door at the end of the hall on the sixth floor. "This," he told me, "has been assigned to you, if it is satisfactory."

I walked into a small entrance hall, furnished in nice French pieces. Beyond this there stretched away a drawing room, a salon, larger than my living room at home. It was carpeted in sapphire blue. The double French windows, running the length of the room and across one end, were hung in heavy oyster white satin, and I lifted them every night to draw the blinds for the blackout. The furniture was upholstered in pale blue and palest lemon-yellow. The clerk led me through this to a small dining room beyond, done in gray and white, and on the other side of that a white kitchen. Then he retraced our steps. "This is the way upstairs," he said, and pointed to a delicate curving iron stairway at the end of the drawing room nearest the entrance hall. From an upstairs hall we went into a large dressing room, all lush peach, mirrors, and lights. A bathroom in sea-foam green was beyond this, and on the far side of the bathroom, my bedroom.

"I hope this will be satisfactory?" the clerk asked anxiously.

I nodded.

"Your apartment, Miss Skinner," he went on, "is on the fifth floor."

We followed him without a word to the fifth floor, and still without a word through the apartment of Miss Skinner, which was a trifle larger than mine, boasting an extra dressing room on the first floor, a balcony off her bedroom, and a Murphy bed which let down incongruously into the middle of the Louis XIV salon.

"Would this," the clerk inquired even more anxiously, "be suitable for Miss Skinner?"

Miss Skinner, with a vacant smile on her face and wave of her hand, indicated mutely that it would. And the clerk departed, bowing.

"Do you think," Cornelia inquired faintly several moments later, "that we ought to telephone Mr. Dozier at Paramount and tell him we are here?"

We had been standing stark still in the center of the drawing room just as the clerk had left us, looking round and round.

She went way down to the telephone, plunging again into her bag for the slip of paper which carried the name of the Paramount executive. Once she had found it, she put through the call. A moment later she read the card again, and turned to me incredulously. "They say," she repeated, "there is no Mr. Dozier. Do you suppose we are calling the wrong company?"

I said that was nonsense. We had sold the book to Paramount. We ought to know where we had sold it.

"Well," she answered. "they say there is no Mr. Dozier at Paramount."

Perhaps they couldn't hear her. I said to spell it. And she did. A curious look came into her face. "May I speak to him?" she asked, and then she covered the mouthpiece again and turned to me. "There is no Mr. Dozier," she said. "It's pronounced D-O-S-H-E-R, and his first name is Bill."

I asked if they seemed to know our names. She said she was not sure but at least they were going to let her speak to him. However his name was pronounced, I still pictured him as small, wiry, highly nervous, and excitable—a flame of creative energy, intolerant of delay or obstacle in anyone else. I urged her to tell him that we could come out right away. I wanted him to realize at the outset that we, too, were consumed with driving energy.

Cornelia was talking to him by this time. "Oh, thank you very much. I'm sure we shall have no trouble," she concluded and hung up the receiver.

I wanted to know why he thought we might have trou-

FROM AN UPSTAIRS HALL WE WENT INTO A LARGE
DRESSING ROOM, ALL LUSH PEACH, MIRRORS, AND LIGHTS.
A BATHROOM IN SEA-FOAM GREEN WAS BEYOND THIS,
AND ON THE FAR SIDE OF THE BATHROOM, MY BEDROOM.

ble. Was he afraid our temperaments would clash? She said that he was afraid we might have difficulty in getting a taxi, and that if we did, tomorrow would do just as well for us to come out to the studio. I asked bleakly if she were sure he wasn't in any hurry for us.

She was sure.

We decided that a very stylish lunch might help to restore our self-confidence, and I went back to my apartment to make myself as chic as possible.

"This hotel does not serve lunch," the clerk told us when we met downstairs at the desk, "only breakfast and dinner because of the servant problem."

I suggested other restaurants of which we had heard. "Oh no," he told us, "they wouldn't do, they're too far away, and you can't get a taxi for at least three quarters of an hour. I know, because I have been trying to get one for another guest. The best thing for you to do is to go to that drugstore across the street on the corner. It's awfully nice," he added. "Almost everybody goes there. The lady cooks the food herself."

We sat on high stools at the counter. I had lamb stew; Cornelia had a chicken pie. I was wearing over my suit a fur cape of baum marten which a friend had insisted on lending to me for the trip to give me more style in the glamorous surroundings of Hollywood. The woman who did the cooking said she would be glad to take care of it

WE SAT ON HIGH STOOLS AT THE COUNTER. I HAD LAMB
STEW; CORNELIA HAD A CHICKEN PIE. I WAS WEARING
OVER MY SUIT A FUR CAPE OF BAUM MARTEN WHICH A
FRIEND HAD INSISTED ON LENDING ME.

for me while I ate because it kept slipping back off my shoulders to the floor and I had to climb down from the stool each time to replace it. So she wedged it between the vanilla and chocolate knobs of the soda fountain.

Chapter Two

We said very little on the way to the studio. Too rapidly
for comfort, the moment was approaching when we should
confront the dynamic Mr. Dozier and be judged. But we
were abruptly distracted, as we rounded a corner, by the
sight, immediately ahead, of about an acre of somber
black canvas three or four stories high, mournfully slap-
ping the air. It looked like the draperies hung occasionally
in front of a police station, only enlarged almost to in-
finity. I pointed it out to Cornelia and asked in a whisper
who, did she think, was dead.

The driver heard me. "Nobody's dead. That's a Cecil B.
de Mille production," he said, "screened off with those
drapes. And," he added proudly, "he can put up the god-
damnedest sets of anybody in this business."

Cornelia and I nodded our heads in agreement. This was
the first set of any kind which I had seen, but it seemed impossible that there could be anything to eclipse it.

The taxi driver stopped the car a few yards beyond.
"Here you are, *girls*," he said, and that term was the first
cheering word of the day. "This is Paramount."

We paid him, and after he had driven away, I still stood

on the sidewalk, looking up at my first motion picture studio. Cornelia moved on serenely. She had, after all, been in a motion picture studio at the age of fourteen and played a part with her father in the picture *Kismet*. Moreover, I think she felt that this was, however remotely, related to the theatre, and the theatre is home and family to her. But it is not even a distant connection of mine.

I may be prejudiced about Paramount because it is now my alma mater, but to me it has more charm than the other studios. The buildings are of cream plaster, low, unpretentious in design, and they extend the length of perhaps two blocks. There is no magnificent approach; the entrance to the office is immediately off the sidewalk, the severe façade of the building being set back a little from the pavement with a strip of lawn and a row of oleanders between. At one side of this entrance there is a driveway from the street. Large double iron gates block it and a watchman is on guard there.

Cornelia inquired from the doorway if I were coming, and I went up the steps, grateful that there were so few because my nervousness made me muscularly a little weak. The doors opened into a reception hall not unlike that at the dentist's or doctor's except that no reading matter was provided. But behind a glass enclosed desk, instead of the nurse, a policeman sat, fully and conspicuously equipped with what seemed to me a great many firearms and other weapons. I thought it unlikely that he should be the reception clerk, but he was—filling in appointment sheets and tending the switchboard as competently as any receptionist, except that he had to bend forward a little stiffly because of the encumbrances around his waist.

Cornelia asked if we might see Mr. Dozier, being careful to pronounce it "Dosher" this time.

"I'll see," the armed force answered. And then he grinned. "Are you girls Skinner and Kimbrough?" he asked eagerly.

We both nodded, too surprised to answer, but I was pleased. I should have liked to go around behind his screen, and pull up a chair to have a good talk with him—he seemed now so cozy and friendly. But other calls came in and Cornelia and I retreated to the bench to wait for our summons, exchanging a surreptitious smile at having heard our own names. After a few minutes the receptionist knocked on the window and pointed with his thumb toward a door on the right. We hurried over, and he put his face down to the opening at the bottom of the window. "Go on in," he said, "Mr. Dozier will be along pretty soon." I asked him where we were to go and he waved reassuringly. "Along that corridor, about the third door down."

We knocked hesitantly on about the third door, and a woman's voice told us to come right in. I did not, of course, know what her name was, but she was either Mr. Dozier's secretary or assistant, very young, very chic, and very friendly. I was beginning to be conscious of this quality everywhere—at the drugstore, in the taxi—a warm reaching out toward another human being, and a complete lack of strangeness, as if the line between a stranger and a friend were scarcely discernible.

"Just sit right down," the chic young hostess invited us. "Mr. Dozier will be here any minute. Will you excuse me if I leave you? I have to see Miss . . ." And she mentioned some one's name as if it were another friend of ours, and the fact of our not having met, unimportant.

Left alone, Cornelia and I looked around us a little furtively. We did not want anyone to come in unexpectedly and find us gawking, Cornelia whispered.

This outer office was of moderate size, furnished with the conventional office furniture, but the walls were hung with photographs, not of motion picture stars, but of landscapes or still life, superb pieces of photography, beautifully mounted and framed—obviously treated like very choice paintings. I told Cornelia that I felt that this was somehow symbolic—this glorification of the photograph—and that a collection of pictures could quite well be a collection of photographs—why not?—and that probably these men knew as much about the merits of a good picture in this medium as another collector would of a painting. I thought, I went on, warming up to the development of this idea, that it was a very good omen for the motion picture industry if you idealized photographs as pictorial art.

Cornelia broke in. "I have a stiff neck," she said. "I knew I ought not to sit in front of an electric fan. It gives me a stiff neck in five minutes."

I was incredulous. I never heard, I told her, of anyone's getting a stiff neck in so short a time. It comes on overnight, I said, and you wake up with it in the morning.

"I don't time mine," she snapped, "and I don't have to wake up to know whether I have it or not. I've got it right now."

I suggested that we change places and that we shut off the fan, but the damage was done. A voice called out from the inner office, "Come on in, girls." And Cornelia, with a despairing slew of her eyes toward me, swept through the door, her head cocked on one side like a robin's. Mr. Dozier, that Gallic flame of passionate energy, was tall, loose jointed, good looking, a little shy, and Scotch. He leaned back in his chair, smiling at us, and asked if we had had a comfortable trip out. Cornelia, sitting gingerly on the edge of her chair because she dared not move her head, said that we had been very comfortable indeed. She looked, at the moment, as if she had never been comfortable in her life. By this time even her mouth was set, lest, if she expanded it, her head might move. She still looked bird-like with her head tilted, but her face had become overcast with a granite expression reminiscent of Grant Wood's *American Gothic*.

Mr. Dozier said that his secretary would show us our

offices presently, that we could work there or at home, whichever we pleased, that Sheridan Gibney was to be the producer, and that we were to work with him on the script, and was there anything he could do for us. I remembered how difficult it was to find a taxi so I asked Mr. Dozier how we could get home. He seemed somewhat at a loss at this, but said after a minute he supposed the man at the desk would take care of it. Then he turned us over to his secretary, and said he would see us soon again.

We followed her back along the corridor and through a door behind the arsenal at the window. I had thought this door would lead us into another wing of the building and was totally unprepared to step through it on to a large inner court of green lawn, enclosed on all sides by charming low buildings. We turned to the right and entered one of these.

"This is the writers' building," our guide told us, and took us down the corridor to the elevator. "You have to run it yourself," she explained, and showed us how to push the buttons. That was the first and last time I achieved my destination in one trip. During the weeks that followed, other people came and went, seemingly under their own control. I never once stepped into it and pushed a button that another button was not pushed simultaneously, and I was drawn inexorably in whichever direction was counter to my intention. My record was made on the day when, endeavoring to go out to lunch, I

reappeared three times on the fourth floor, to the astonished delight of Irene, the telephone operator there.

This time we rose, emerged at the fourth floor, went
down to the end of the corridor, and were shown into a
corner office and the room adjoining. These were both to
be ours, we were told, and I noted with particular pleasure that each boasted a luxurious couch. Our guide left us
and Cornelia and I counted off, and drew an office, hers
the corner one and mine next to it with a connecting door
between.

We sat down at our respective desks, opened all the
drawers, called back and forth to each other our pleasure
at the writing paper with Paramount Studios and address
and telephone number stamped upon it, our amazement
at the bulk of the studio inter-office directory, and our con-
jectures about who else was in the writers' building. Then
I went over to my window and talked to her about what I
could see. She told me in turn what she could see from
hers. After that we went back to our desks, and I counted
the number of pencils in the top right-hand drawer. When
I had finished that, I went to the connecting door of our
offices and suggested tentatively that unless she thought
there was something urgent we ought to do, I guessed I
would write a letter to my twins.

"That's what I'm doing," she said, "writing a letter to
Dickie."

So I went back and wrote a letter to each of the twins

on the Paramount stationery. I carried the letters into Cornelia's office and found she had finished, too.

I asked if she thought we had done enough for today. She thought we had. "But please don't," she added, "ask anybody else how we're to get home." I was quite surprised at this. "Well," she went on, "maybe you don't know it, but every person we've seen since we got here you've asked to tell us how we could get home. Mr. Dozier looked very startled. After all, you've just come, and besides it isn't exactly his job as an executive to blow the whistle for a taxi for you."

That seemed to me unfair. They had all been eager to do something for us and had kept pleading with us to let them know what they could do; I thought it was more friendly to give them something. The only thing I could think of was how to get a taxi, and I didn't really know how we did get one. Cornelia answered that she didn't know either. "But this time we're not going to find out. We're going to walk. I will not ask another person today to show us how to get home. It's just a step anyway."

It was a step of about an hour and a half.

As we entered the hotel wearily, a man crossed the lobby just ahead of us. I called out and hurried after him. A few minutes later we came back together to Cornelia, standing as if she were playing "Still Pond—no more moving," and I introduced Norman Brock, who was an old friend from Philadelphia. He broke in eagerly to say that he had heard we were coming, and would we dine with him and a friend, Walter Van Pelt, if we were not too tired. Cornelia came out of "Still Pond" with a rush. "I'm not a bit tired. Are you, Emily?" I agreed that I was not, and it was settled that we would meet downstairs at eight-thirty.

"Don't dress," Norman called after us as we got into the elevator. "Remember, this is not Philadelphia—it's Hollywood."

"I thought you were picking him up," Cornelia muttered in the elevator. "I was horrified. It made me stiff as a board. It seemed so undignified at our age." I told her indignantly that I had never picked anyone up at any age. "You probably didn't," she said aloud, as she left the elevator. "You were an awful sap."

We were both over-tired.

A great bond between Norman Brock and me is our love of food. His is the natural birthright of anyone from Philadelphia. Mine is the passion of one to whom love has come late. In my native state of Indiana food is cooked too long and with too much water. I was a grown girl, too, before I discovered that carrots and peas did not have to be imbedded in paste. He had, he said, as we got to his car, increased his collection of cookbooks, and invited me to stop in to see them when we got back. I asked him if he had a kitchen in his apartment at the hotel, where he could try out some of these things. He said oh no, but he did not mind that; he liked to read recipes the way you read any other kind of literature.

It must have been nearly nine, but it was still dusk when we drove through the gate. "This is Lucey's," Walter said as we stood on the step waiting for Norman to park the car. "It's just around the corner from Paramount, and not far from the hotel." Just an hour and a half's step, I could have told him. The air was chilly and I was glad I had worn my fur cape, yet the smells were heavy and sweet, like midsummer.

We went into the bar first. There were no steps. It was just over the threshold from the garden. I am always aware, in California, with fresh surprise and pleasure, how close and low to a garden almost every building tries to be. Sitting on a stool next to him, I had my first really good look at Norman's friend. I do not know what a typical Hollywood citizen is, but he seemed to me not like anyone I might have met either in the Middle West nor in the East, and yet there was certainly nothing bizarre in his appearance. It was only that he was more tanned than our change of seasons gives time for, and his eyes, which were as bright a blue as an aquamarine, were squinted up a little, not in the manner of people who ought to wear glasses, but of people who look at the sun a great deal and never wear glasses at all. His hair was very white, yet I have no faintest idea of his age because he was wiry and compact and in the kind of athletic trim which requires three hundred and sixty-five days a year to maintain. He wore a dark blue suit with a light blue sweater under the coat instead of a waistcoat. In all the time I was out there I never saw him wear an overcoat, and I never saw him without a sweater under the coat of his suit. And I never saw him wear a hat. "I buy a hat," he complained one time, "and I carry it, but I always leave it and then I have to go buy another. I guess it's because I don't wear them."

He asked what I would have to drink, and I apologized because I drink only beer. I knew it was peculiar. He was delighted. "Now that's what I like—drink what you want, and stick to it." He called to the bartender, "This lady drinks only beer and I want her to find out what the best beer is."

The bartender leaned over sympathetically toward me. "Can't you drink anything else?"

During the years in Philadelphia, I had forgotten about this brand of little-town folksiness, but all day the Hollywood kind had carried me back to Indiana, and I responded to it. Liquor, I explained, did not make me tight or anything unfortunate like that—it just did not agree with me—except beer.

"You don't say!" the barkeeper marveled. "Matter of fact, I had a cousin like that, lived in Utah, couldn't touch a drop, upset his digestion something awful. He could drink beer, too, though, just the same as you—must be the malt makes it set all right."

Carta Blanca, they decided, was as good as any. It was a Mexican light beer. Van Merritt was fine, too,—like Dutch beer. You couldn't get it everywhere. We could have gone on with this indefinitely, but Norman by now was doing a schottische of agitation between the bar and the dining room, where he had already steered Cornelia. So we left the barkeeper with reluctance and my regards to his cousin in Utah, and joined the others at the table.

The dinner was wonderful. We began with cold cracked crab, although Cornelia was doubtful about eating sea-food so far away from the ocean. "I don't," she explained kindly to Walter Van Pelt in order not to hurt his feelings, "eat it even so far west as Chicago."

Walter closed his eyes a moment, and then said gently, "There is another ocean, you know, the Pacific, *right here.* Cracked crab comes from the Pacific; you can't even get it in the Atlantic Ocean."

I do not think I am always a malicious woman, but I was exalted that she, an old geography expert, could be a provincial New Yorker. If you come from the Middle West, like me, you are at least impartial about the oceans. However, we were back at the Atlantic seaboard almost immediately.

"They have eastern beef here," Norman confided in a solemn whisper.

I asked if eastern beef were better than western. And it was Norman's turn to look pained.

"All the good beef," he explained reverently, "comes from the East."

I was incredulous that with all those acres for cattle in Texas, the beef wasn't good.

"Not until it is shipped East to fatten. Then it comes back here, but it is eastern beef by that time."

It seemed to me another evidence of geographic undependability, but by that time we were eating the beef, and it was delicious, wherever it came from.

We stopped talking about food then, and turned to motion pictures. Walter Van Pelt knew everyone in the movie world, and he represented an aspect of it which I thought unusual. If some one, he explained, happened on a good script, brought it to him and he liked it, he would get the production financed, round up a group of actors, hire a producer and a director, and then rent a studio, or a portion of one, not in use. Then they would move in, set up camp like gypsies, produce their picture, fold up their tents, and depart again. They borrowed everything—the people, the sets, the costumes, and the place in which to work.

He asked if we should like to meet Hedda Hopper, the famous columnist, and one of the people I was most curi-

ous to see. What day then would we be free for lunch?
Since neither Cornelia nor I had any engagements whatsoever for the following five weeks until we returned East
again, we were able to promise our time for luncheon the
following week. He immediately signalled a waiter and
asked for a telephone. I watched spellbound while he
thumbed over the pages of his private directory, nearly
as large as the telephone book of Muncie, Indiana, and
found Hedda's number.

There is a Hollywood telephone directory printed and
published, but perhaps the names and numbers in it are
just made up by the city officials to spare them the embarrassment of not having a publication like other towns.
During the entire time I was there I met only one person whose name, address, and number were listed. That
was Nina Koshetz. No, two people; Ray Redman was
listed, too. As far as I know, they were the only authentic
ones in the whole directory. I do know people in New
York whose names are not listed, but I also know a good
many whose names are. But, except for Nina and Ray
Hollywood's was a closed book to me. Walter found
Hedda's number in his own list, telephoned her from the
table, and made an engagement for us all to lunch together ten days later.

We finished dinner, and the waiter and head-waiter,
who had been in and out of the conversation all evening,
said good-bye to us with such seeming regret at the part-

ing of old friends that I explained we would be back the next week for lunch. Oh yes, they said, Miss Hopper came there often. She was a lovely lady and we would enjoy meeting her. I am sure it was not inquisitiveness, but interest which made them aware of everything that had gone on, but it *was* different from our feeling for privacy in the East.

On the way home Norman asked if we would mind going around by way of Hollywood Boulevard. Inasmuch as we did not know one boulevard from another, we assured him that we had no favorite way. But Walter began to chuckle. "He has to get his evening paper there. Every night he gets his car out, or walks a mile, so he can get his paper at that place."

Norman looked surprised. He said, "Why, I bought my paper there the first night I got here and I don't like changing around." There was the very essence of Philadelphia. It brought me with a stab, close to home, and I thought again how misleading geography is.

Chapter Three

We got a taxi the next morning to take us to the studio. It was driven by a woman. I found later that most of the drivers were women, and all of them friendly. They would come inside the building to get us, and walk back to the taxi, talking all the way, asking with interest where we were from and how long we had been there. And they themselves invariably came from some other part of the country, to which they would refer wistfully, always declaring that Hollywood was the place to live in, and they wouldn't go back for anything—only they would just like to make a visit some time.

The armored receptionist had cards waiting for us. "These are your identification tickets," he said. "Be sure to keep them with you in case there should be some substitute here who wouldn't let you in." I may receive something some day which will give me a greater sense of importance than that entry card, but I cannot think what it would be.

Sheridan Gibney telephoned us soon after we reached our office. Would we, he asked, have lunch with him at the Commissary at one o'clock. He would meet us downstairs. In the meantime we might like to begin thinking about some dialogue.

Cornelia asked, when she had hung up the telephone, if I thought we ought to get an engagement book. We had two engagements now, lunch today and next week.

Since we had never been side by side to collaborate on the book, we did not know just how to start off. But Cornelia sat down at the typewriter, and I in a big armchair by the window. We talked and then she wrote. But in a few minutes I suggested that we change places. I am sure that Cornelia is as efficient on the typewriter as she is at everything she does, and I know that I am unsound about margins, and letters piled on top of each other. But at least my contact with the machine is not that of a miniature painter—one delicate stroke at a time, and a careful scrutiny of what it has accomplished.

She did not sit down while I typed. She could think better, she said, if she walked about. Her walking led her to the window, and there she paused for a long time. I thought she was working out a line over which we had been wrestling, and I scarcely dared breathe, lest I jar the lovely prose that was being shaped. Finally she spoke. "Bob Hope," she said, "is riding this way on a bicycle." I suggested with some bitterness that perhaps she'd like to stop work and go down to meet him, but she said, no, she would like only to throw him a rose.

We did a little dialogue on and off during the rest of the

morning, but it did not read smoothly. I preferred her at the window, even with the vapors, to miniature painting. Still, it was hard to keep the train of thought we had supposedly been hired to establish, when she was saying, "I don't know whether you're interested, but Ginger Rogers is going by. She is lovely looking. What on earth has she got on—a fur skirt?"

We both hung out the window at that, though I was jeering. How could she identify Ginger Rogers and fur from four stories up?

"Because I'm far sighted," she retorted, "like an eagle." And sure enough, it was Ginger Rogers. At least it was my impression of Ginger Rogers from four stories up, and certainly my impression of a fur skirt. "It's mink," Cornelia announced from her eagle vantage. "It's an evening dress with a mink skirt."

I maintain that even for Hollywood that is quite a fair sight to see in the blazing midday sun—Bob Hope on a bicycle, and a mink-skirted evening dress.

We just puttered after that. Everything we thought of seemed flat. We were ravenously hungry, too, but we thought it a little over-eager to telephone Sheridan to ask if he could take us to lunch earlier. When he did telephone that he was waiting downstairs, we had had our hats, coats, and gloves on for some time. We told him what we had seen, but he was not impressed. "Bob is working on *Let's Face It*, and Ginger is doing *Lady in the*

Dark. I thought you might like to stroll over after lunch and see them. That mink skirt of Ginger's set the front office back five thousand dollars."

I scarcely noticed where we were walking. We were about to see movie actors at work, and no one thought either a mink skirt or five thousand dollars odd, although they were neither of them every day commodities to me. Then I was aware that we were in a strange part of town. There was a drug store on the corner which we were approaching, and a men's clothing store next to it. I could see a display of sporting goods in the window of the store beyond, and the unmistakable front of a bar on our side of the street. They seemed down at the heel, and the neighborhood tough, although I could not have said exactly why. I told Sheridan that I thought Paramount Studios owned this whole area. He was talking to Cornelia and answered a little abstractedly that certainly it did. Then he turned back to me with a second thought. "This is a movie set," he said. "Did you think it was real?"

I can only say that, although I was aware that we might conceivably at a motion picture studio see a set for a motion picture, I had no idea that a set could look like that. I have seen them from back stage in the theatre —I think I have heard Cornelia call them "flats"—and that is what I thought I should see—flat pieces representing very accurately the facade of a house or building. But these make-believe buildings had all the dimensions that

47

any buildings require, and they looked, furthermore, as if they had been there a long time, built on good foundations, too, not propped up.

Sheridan was comforting. "A visitor on the lot last week," he said, "banged on the counter in that drug store to get some one to sell him a package of cigarettes. He thought the clerk was in the back somewhere."

We walked to the end of the block, turned a corner, and were in a street of charming Georgian houses. I recovered a little of my self confidence, and told Sheridan that at least I could recognize this as a set. I should have known it at once. It had the look of the theatre about it—it was so perfect. But the other street looked LIVED in.

THIS was real, he said. They were offices of the studio. A lot of the offices and buildings for various departments were built on little streets like this, and in a definite period, so that they could be used in pictures, and they *were* used all the time.

Behind the curtained windows I heard the rattle of typewriters. We moved on into a block of Queen Anne residences. Offices, I presumed. And Sheridan said they were. But it was Cornelia of the eagle eye who saw that the peeling stucco up near the eaves was done with red paint to look like brickwork underneath, and that the old timbers were painted, too.

The Commissary was genuine, and of no period—just a

48

long, one-story building of pink plaster, with bright pink doors. Inside, it was crowded, and Sheridan said we should have to wait a few minutes for a table.

But at that moment I spotted one. It was against the wall, near the door, and I could quite see how it would be overlooked. I hurried ahead before anyone else could seize it, and I did not look back to see if they were following, but squeezed myself into the place against the wall. It was the hardest to reach, but it left the more accessible ones for the laggards. At the very instant that I actually sat down, the noise in the room died away as if a candle snuffer had been clamped over it. I looked for Cornelia and Sheridan, and saw them standing several tables away. They had evidently stopped to speak to someone. But Cornelia caught my eye and put her hand up to her face in shame, shaking her head. Out of the hush, a waitress tiptoed up to me.

"Miss," she said in a whisper that blew all over the room, "that's Mr. Cecil B. de Mille's seat, and there hasn't been any one but him sat in it for fifteen years."

People began talking again almost at once, but I think every eye in the room watched me push and scramble out and all the way down the room to my comrades, until I found shelter at a table in the farthest corner.

All the girls sitting near us were in slacks. Stenographers and clerks, Sheridan said. You could, he said, tell from the difference in make-up that they were not

49

actresses. I couldn't. Their hair-dos were another point of interest. I learned later that a kind of lacquer made possible their four and five inch pompadours. They carry the lacquer around in a bottle, and, like using a compact, pour out a little of this jelly into the palm of the hand and rub it up their hair. Frequently the back of the coiffure behind the pompadour was braided in two stiff pigtails, not down the back, but out over each shoulder. The ends were tied with bright ribbons and long streamers, or the ribbons were wound in and out of the braids, like the manes of Percherons at county fairs. The hair dyes, too, were as imaginative as the hair-dos. One girl from the costume department had achieved a shade only a little off shocking pink, and I can see it now in front of me like the blobs of lights that stay in the air after a flashlight picture has been taken. In our traveling suits, hats, and gloves, Cornelia and I were period pieces.

Of course *Lady in the Dark* is not filmed every day, although its director, when I asked him, said he thought he had begun it when a small boy, and would not live to see its completion. Perhaps when that is not in production, one will not see people lunching there in gold clothes, face, hands, arms, and hair; but I am sure they will have been replaced by other arresting flights of fancy. They stood in line at the buffet table, these golden creatures, laughing and talking among themselves, and it was an eerie sight.

Sheridan called out, "Oh Ray!" And one of them fell out of line and came over to our table. "This is Ray Milland," Sheridan explained. I should have thought I might have identified Ray Milland at sight, but a change of complexion is a wonderful disguise.

Cornelia and I had both seen *Lady in the Dark* in New York,—the play by Moss Hart, with Gertrude Lawrence as the magazine editor heroine. She was, we remembered, psychoanalyzed, accompanied by music, to a happy and romantic ending. But we could not place the gold hair, hands and faces. Ray explained that they were for the wedding sequence, which was one of the dream sequences. And he invited us to watch it taken.

When he had gone, we asked Sheridan about the people around us. He said that practically everybody was there. I identified Dorothy Lamour, Victor Moore, Zasu Pitts, and Bing Crosby, and was somewhat exhilarated by my own acumen. But Sheridan could not verify it. He didn't, he said, know many of the actors by sight. However, his wife and twelve-year-old daughter did, he added, with pride. And he did know almost everyone who wasn't an actor. "Those are some of the executives at that table in the middle of the room. That's Y. Frank Freeman, the vice-president of the company." He pointed to a short, compact, middle-aged man, with pince nez, and a kindly smile for everyone who passed the table.

I grabbed Sheridan's arm. I knew, I told him, the man

on Mr. Freeman's right—he was the director in the Greek plays that Margaret Anglin gave at Berkeley, and I was in them. I told all about how my family had taken a house in Berkeley that year, and I had gotten into the Greek plays by a fluke. And I gave a line-by-line description of what the director and Miss Anglin—and I—did. His name was Gustav Von Seyfertitz and he was an Austrian.

Sheridan Gibney is a gentleman, and a patient man. He heard me all the way through the *Iphigenia,* the *Medea,* and the *Electra,* and then he said, "This man's name is George Brown and he is the head of the publicity department here."

I let the others talk then, and Cornelia asked if Sheridan had said that Mr. Freeman's first name was *Why.* He said no, but that people always asked that. It was Y, and stood for Young—just a toss-up whether you preferred being called Young Frank or Why Frank. Cornelia also wanted to know, a little self-consciously and hopefully, if this were the special dining room for the executives and stars—and writers. Not in the least, Sheridan said. It was for any one, and there was no special place, except, he coughed apologetically, Mr. de Mille's seat. A group of writers sat at one big table in a smaller room at one side, but that was because they played a game called The Word Game, every day, and were so quarrelsome over it, that they were asked to go there. And everybody had the same menu, too. There was no special big de luxe lunch.

If you ordered at the table, it was a little more expensive than the buffet. But the food there was delicious; you could have everything on the table, and come back for more—most people preferred it. The company lost money, but he had heard the executives say that they liked to make sure that the extras, when they were working here, got one big substantial meal a day.

The room emptied of the golden beauties, and Sheridan suggested that we go over to see if their sequence was being shot. I said that I did not see how there could be any doubt about it, since they were all in costume and in that elaborate make-up. That meant absolutely nothing he told us. You had to get them there at six in the morning, because it took so long to get the make-up put on properly, and the costumes, but if things didn't go right —and there were more things to go wrong than any one could count—you might have them around like that for days without taking a single shot. I asked if that were not terribly expensive, and he said, yes, it was.

We were passing large buildings that looked like warehouses. Each one carried a sign, "Stage 9," "Stage 13," and so forth. The numbers were not in any sort of order and Sheridan said they were numbered according to when they were built, not where they stood. So Stage 9 was the ninth stage built, and when they got to building thirteen, probably the best place for it was next to nine.

Along the side of one of the stages, we came upon a

miniature lake. I wish we had never seen it. But we stopped because it looked so interesting. It was not, as a matter of fact, very miniature. At least it was, I should say, about two hundred feet square. Along the shore on one side was a village, however, that was really diminutive. The thatched huts were not more than two feet high and there were palm trees to scale. Tiny pieces of wash, also to scale, hung on the line, and a sandy beach in front went down to a series of little piers. On the lake itself there were boats, also small, and these were filled with toy figures dressed in army uniform and a few in nurses', all, as far as we could see, correct to the tiniest line indicating braid on a cuff.

This was the escape from Bataan, Sheridan explained, for *So Proudly We Hail.* I thought the little episodes and sights of the day so far had dulled any sensation of surprise, but it came alive over this. Cornelia was as incredulous as I, so that when Sheridan asked if we should like to stay and see it actually done, instead of going on to *Lady in the Dark*, she was all in favor of it.

Facing the little village was a complicated and mysterious looking device, a wind machine we were told, which would make waves for the boats to ride. When the scene was "blown up," and that meant enlarged, the life-sized boats, filled with life-sized men and nurses, would be seen getting away from the village in the distance, over a very rough sea. Then when a close-up was shown of the characters in the picture, they would actually be on this same lake in an authentic boat and the wind machine turned on harder, I suppose, and making life-sized waves.

At the end of the lake nearest us, a really super-colossal cyclorama was hung on a framework. It represented the sky and was a beautiful job of painting. We were told that the real sky was almost never used, because it looked "phony." In front of the cyclorama was what in the theatre is called a profile piece. I do not know what the motion picture linguists call it, but it was a silhouette of the mountains of Bataan. Between it and the cyclorama a cat-walk had been put down, and we started across it. I was behind the other two because I had been looking at a detail on the shore and had not noticed them leave. As I got midway I saw the wind machine begin to revolve and the boats move off from the docks. I could not imagine what made them go until I saw that men wading around in hip boots were holding one end of a long wire, and that the other end was fast to the bow of each of these boats, one man to a boat, and each with a separate and rehearsed course to follow. A group of people at the other end on the shore, facing me, seemed to be made up of the directors or head mechanics. I was not paying attention to them; I was only conscious that there was a group there.

Whistles blew and bells rang. People shouted. The noise was deafening. It had been like that wherever we went. Scenery trucks passing us on our way to lunch had blown and drivers had yelled. Everything, I thought, was done very violently out here, as if each detail had to be dramatized. No restraint, as there is in the East. And then I saw that the men at the other end were waving at me, and I melted. For all our quiet, we had not their warmth, their eye out for a stranger, and their immediate instinct to make him feel one of them. I waved back at them happily.

The little boats moved out, each following its own pattern, with no crossing of wires and in perfect timing. I looked up from them to the men at the far end of the lake, and clasped my hands at them in the prize fighter's gesture of greeting and congratulation, calling that it was wonderful. They answered something which I could not hear, but it was enthusiastic. I waved back. "It's lovely to be here." I could not think of anything appreciative enough to say.

The men in the hip boots came wading toward me, dragging their wires behind them, and when they got quite near I could hear what they were yelling. I do not know how soon it came over me that it was all at me— and not because I had come to Hollywood and they were glad, but because I was standing in the middle of the picture and they were wild. But when it did reach my understanding, I dropped to the crouch of a sprinter and made my way across to Sheridan and Cornelia. They had

I WAVED BACK. "IT'S LOVELY TO BE HERE." I COULD NOT
THINK OF ANYTHING APPRECIATIVE ENOUGH TO SAY.

been yelling at me, too, all the time, imploring me to get out of the way and join them, but in the general din I had not distinguished their pleas.

The next night when the rushes were shown—and that means the film taken the day before—above the distant mountain tops of Bataan, I was told, rose the upper half of Miss Kimbrough, brooding and engrossed on the evacuation. And since the scene had been blown up to life size, Miss Kimbrough was blown up to proportion beyond reason, and a sinister sight. Quite a number of feet, they told me, too, had been shot before I was noticed against the sky, so the cost was considerable.

I felt that the whole day one way and another had cost me quite a lot, too, and I wanted no more of it.

Chapter Four

We dressed ourselves up as stylishly as possible for our lunch with Hedda Hopper. Unfortunately it rained, not a gentle mist but a downpour, so that when we arrived at Lucey's without an umbrella and wiped our streaming faces enough to see Walter Van Pelt and Hedda waiting, her first words were, "What on earth made you get so dressed up on this kind of a day?" She had on a white raincoat, and a small, close-fitting, black hat, both so chic that in our oozing finery we looked as if we had not only made our own clothes, but the patterns, too. Her figure is, like the little bear's porridge, just right; her hair is reddish blond, and her eyes are very wide and very blue. I do not know that I am particularly interested in ages, but looking back on the people I met in Hollywood, I realize that I have not the slightest idea or conjecture of the age of any one of them. They all had vitality and warmth.

Hedda's voice is a little husky and her approach very direct. "Well, girls," she said, the moment we were seated, "what have you done? Whom have you met since you got here?"

Cornelia told her with a good deal of embellishment what I had done in the way of getting into the movies, and then she added in a small voice, "We haven't met anybody at the studio except Mr. Dozier the first day, and Sheridan Gibney, of course, our boss."

"Haven't you met any of the writers?" Hedda demanded.

We shook our heads.

Producers? Directors? Publicity? Executives?

We were more and more shamefaced. I said that the gateman knew us. And a man had also come into our office that morning. He wanted us to be assistant air wardens, I thought, but I had not been able to understand his accent very well. He had seemed to say that in an air raid we would meet on the roof. That was our only other engagement.

Hedda was all action. "I'll see about that right away. Have you watched *Lady in the Dark?*"

Cornelia volunteered that we had started to but that I had got into *Bataan* instead. She had heard that no one was let in, anyway.

"They'll let you in," Hedda threatened. "You leave it to me. But why don't your secretaries get you in wherever you want to go?"

We both said, "Secretaries!" blankly. And I echoed that we didn't even have one, let alone referring to a plural.

I added with a firm look at Cornelia that *I* did the typing.

"You mean you've started to work?"

Cornelia told her indignantly that we had written about twelve thousand words. It might not be much but we were certainly working.

Hedda appealed to Walter. "I think they're crazy, or else they're just too innocent to live without protection. Girls," she pleaded with us, "there are writers who don't put a word on paper for a month. There are those who have gone as long as six months without communicating a thought to a typewriter. You'll frighten the front office to death if you start producing right away."

All this time she had nodded and smiled to every person who caught her eye, and every person who came into the room made a point of catching it. But now she reached out and tugged the sleeve of a young man who had come all the way around the room in order to leave the restaurant by way of our table. "Bill," she demanded, "do you know who these two are?"

Bill regretted that he had ever deviated from the straight and narrow exit he might have taken. "Well, now," he began, "I should, I know."

Hedda withered him. "Oh no, there's no reason why you should. They're only two girls out here in your own studio doing their book into a movie for you, hired by you, and brought on from the East."

Bill looked more unhappy. "Why, of course."

"You DON'T know who they are," Hedda thundered, "but you'd better. They're Skinner and Kimbrough," she told him, "and nobody's looked in at them except the air raid warden. At least he's dated them up for the roof, which is more than I can say for anybody else, except Walter here."

It is a test of poise to meet, unflinching, the echoing report of your social failure.

Bill's poise was beautiful. "Why," he announced, "we've been planning a party for both of you. The publicity department is going to give a party." You could see the idea developing. "Yes, sir, we've been talking about it. We're going to have the press and everybody. And you're the first person to be invited, Hedda."

"I'll bet I am," she told him sweetly.

"You bet you are. I didn't recognize you girls by sight, but we're certainly making plans for you. I've got to run along now because I want to get started on lining up some interviews for you. Is everything all right? You being taken care of all right? Getting around all right? I guess you are, to have met Hedda. She's a great girl, isn't she? Well, good-bye now. I'll be seeing you a lot."

Somewhere in this he told us his name, and I thought he said Mr. Bluefish, which I called him until the day before we left for home. Then he confided in the midst of good-bye that his name was Bill Blowitz, in case I should write.

We left the restaurant after Bill's departure. Walter offered to drive us to the Studio, since it was still raining and he was taking Hedda back to her office, so we climbed in behind them.

He stopped at the big iron gates across the driveway, instead of the modest pedestrian entrance to the office. And Hedda said over her shoulder, "Here's the one man you said knew you. I guess I don't have to help you get in to work."

Cornelia whispered to me, "This isn't the gate we've come through before. He won't know us."

We got out and stood beside the car, thanking them, until Hedda said, "Go on, girls, we'll see you safely in."

We laughed faintly. That wasn't at all necessary, we assured her. Just go right on, and thank you again. They still waited, so we walked firmly up to the man at the gate. He bawled at us, "Hey, where do you think you're goin'?"

Cornelia whispered hoarsely, "We work here. We are writers."

"Not to my knowledge you ain't," the guardian told everybody within a quarter of a block. "I never seen you before in my life. Where's your cards?"

We began shuffling and plunging in our bags, finding our railroad ticket stubs, driving license, charge account slips, telephone numbers, letters from the children, but no sign of the identification tickets we had been so proud to receive.

A car door closed and Hedda came up beside us. "What's the matter here?" she said. "Don't you know these girls?"

"No, I don't, Miss Hopper," he told her, "but if you say they're all right, that'll do for me."

She spoke sharply to us. "Stop fumbling in your bags. He knows you now, but if I can find a good reliable keeper for you, I'll let you know."

From that day, I never went through that gate again, and I never overcame my dislike of the watchman.

The next morning I sat in my dining room at breakfast, the sun warm between my shoulders, and the smell of eucalyptus drifting in from the wide open windows behind me. Sounds came in, too, and they nagged at my memory until from far, far back I recognized them. They were spring cleaning noises, and I had not heard them since I was a child in a little town: an underhumming of vacuum cleaners; above it, the thump of rug beating, the clatter of a mop handle on a window sill as the dust is shaken out, the crack of dust cloths out the window, the hammering of screens into place, the squeak of window panes rubbed dry, and the voices of neighbors calling to each other probably about bedrooms and closets still to be done. Cities are quiet about housecleaning, and yet here in this de luxe cosmopolitan hotel the feel of a

CORNELIA WHISPERED HOARSELY, "WE WORK HERE. WE ARE WRITERS." "NOT TO MY KNOWLEDGE YOU AIN'T," THE GUARDIAN TOLD EVERYBODY WITHIN A QUARTER OF A BLOCK. "I NEVER SEEN YOU BEFORE IN MY LIFE. WHERE'S YOUR CARDS?"

little town came up to the sixth floor—a distilled essence of Hollywood.

I turned to Hedda Hopper's column in the Los Angeles paper. It would be even more interesting to read, now that I had met her. It was interesting for more than that.

"Lunched with Cornelia Otis Skinner and Emily Kimbrough," it began. "They had to use all their persuasion to get by the gateman. . . . They were given an office, but they are still doing their own typing. . . . Emily got on the *Bataan* set by mistake; a policeman removed her. . . . Emily seated herself in Cecil de Mille's private chair. . . . Cornelia wants to throw Bob Hope a rose when he goes by on a bicycle. . . . The studio has not found out they are here. . . . However, things will be different now. . . . If they don't write a book on *Alice in Movieland,* I'll chew my pet nail off."

Hedda's column is widely read.

We had no sooner reached our office than the telephones began to ring. Mr. Leisen's secretary was calling to ask if we should like to see the *Lady in the Dark* wedding sequence done on Monday afternoon. Mr. Leisen was the Director. They thought they would be ready for a take then. At three o'clock? That would be lovely. Only she did not say that she was Mr. Leisen's secretary. She said she was Mitch Leisen's. Everyone at Paramount is known by his first name up to one of the chief executives, who is called Buddy. Charlie Brackett told me the first day I met him that people from the East were always surprised at this custom. "Later," he said, "you are not surprised by any name. There is a man on this lot," he added with pride, "who never calls *me* anything but Love Bud."

The publicity department telephoned to say that Mr. Bluefish would like us to have some photographs taken. Could we possibly have them done that afternoon? They hated to rush us, but they were in a hurry to get out some press stories about our having *just* arrived. And when would we give some interviews? We said we had to work, and the voice on the telephone laughed. Oh well, then, we weren't so busy that we could not have some interviews right now. And we did. There were two newspaper reporters in our office within half an hour. And an hour later we were being photographed on a set with Claudette Colbert.

Miss Colbert was working in a picture entitled, *So Proudly We Hail*. She was an army nurse, assisted by those two staunch defenders of the realm, Veronica Lake and Paulette Goddard. Miss Rooks from the publicity department was guiding us—she asked us to call her Lyle— and we stumbled after her into the big warehouse which was as dark as the inside of a boot.

Considering that *terrific* and *colossal* are the root words of the Hollywood vocabulary, *stage* as the word for a building the size of an armory is certainly an irregular noun. I have seen set up in it the entire side and upper deck of a ship, and, for another picture, a broad canal some eight to ten feet deep, into which a man dived and on which a coal barge floated. Behind and along the side of the canal were some buildings and a dock, from the city of Prague. This was occupying only a comparatively small area of the stage. On our first visit, however, when we crept along behind Lyle Rooks there were no sets of any kind—only blackness and emptiness, except for ropes and occasional chairs over which we buckled. We must have rounded a corner somewhere, for suddenly there were a few lights in the distance. And when we came close enough to see, we discovered that a scene was being taken. Claudette Colbert and a young man, her hand in his, stood facing Walter Abel. The army nurse on the right of Miss Colbert was evidently the witness, and Walter Abel a chaplain. He was marrying the couple in the Rock of Corregidor. They all looked worn and shabby in their uniforms, and as we came close enough to see this we heard Walter Abel say these words:

Dear God, we have none of the things which are usually used to solemnize marriage, in this one, except the thing You prize most—sincerity of heart. Somewhere, somehow, on this field of battle amid all the inhumanity, human things happen, too. Amid all the boiling hatred, both righteous and unrighteous, two of your servants, Lord, have found love, and desire to be wed in Thine eyes. Help me, O Lord, in my halting fashion to consecrate this marriage.

68

(*He looks at them.*)

Amid all the fearful things around us, you children saw your future. Whatever has happened has not blurred your vision of one another. And this is true: what you saw in the other will always exist. It is the final truth. I can't seem to say all I feel about you, Janet, and you, John, but I charge you both to re, member that in the end love and loyalty alone will avail.

And now—Wilt thou, John, have this woman to be thy wedded wife, to have and to hold? Wilt thou love her, honor her, comfort her, keep her in sickness and in health, and, forsaking all others, keep her till death do you part?

JOHN

I will.

CHAPLAIN

And wilt thou, Janet, have this man to be thy wedded husband, to have and to hold——

(*He breaks down, unable to go on.*)

JANET (*strongly*)

I will.

CHAPLAIN

I then pronounce you man and wife.

(*They look at each other for a moment.*)

CHAPLAIN

And this much more I do remember: Those whom God hath joined together, let not man put asunder.

(*He looks up.*)

Be merciful, God.

69

I think that I remember sounds more vividly and longer than I do the things which I see, and I think that I shall never forget that prose as it came in a voice scarcely above a whisper—one speaks very low for the microphone —but with the impact of a great actor upon it. The moving words came out of a tiny lighted corner of a vast, silent, empty building and only we three were listening. In a very little while, of course, millions of people would hear them. I hoped they would listen to them, too.

The scene ended, and Walter Abel came over to speak to us. He sensed our mood at once, and said quietly, "That's a beautifully written scene, isn't it? Movie audiences don't pay very much attention to the writing behind a picture. I hope they will listen to what Allen Scott says here."

I thought of how the name of the writer, Allen Scott, would be presented when the picture came before the public, somewhere along with the assistant photographer and the assistant to the assistant sound recorder, and all that long table of names which no one in the audience ever has the patience or the time to read. Playwrights are identified, but the writer of a motion picture is just another of the sound effects.

Miss Colbert had been going over some detail with the director, but as she turned to leave the set, she caught sight of us and came running across. "Why, Cornelia Skinner," she said, "how wonderful. I heard you were coming, but I didn't know you were on the lot. I'm **so** flattered that you came over to see our picture."

She is lovely looking—slim, wide-eyed; and the shape of her face is like a child's. I think it is because her cheeks are little round knobs, as if she were carrying nuts like a squirrel. She was friendly and cordial to me, but she turned back with delight to Cornelia and asked if she re-membered the play they had been in together.

Cornelia had told me that they had appeared in *The Wild Westcotts,* that it was Claudette's first part, and that the two of them had roomed together on tour. She said she had always remembered Claudette's beautiful un-derwear and was so impressed when Claudette had told her she made it herself—all her clothes, as a matter of fact, and her hats. Miss Colbert told us firmly, "I'd still make them if I had time. I could make better hats right now than the ones I buy." Then she admitted that what *she* remembered particularly were Cornelia's bath salts. She had thought they made the most luxurious atmos-phere she had ever been in during her life, and was sure it was true, too. Her family was poor, she said, and very thrifty French. She'd never even seen bath salts before in her life, but she made up her mind that she'd never stop working until she could have them herself. She looked down at her crumpled uniform and added, "I could use them right now, too. I'm always being cast in

71

muddy pictures, but this is the muddiest. I'm practically never clean."

A photographer from the publicity department reported to Miss Rooks and she asked us to pose for him. I considered this quite an important moment and was inordinately pleased. But I whispered to Cornelia that I thought the photographer was not using enough light. Cornelia breathed back at me in some agitation that she would count it a personal favor if I would not interfere with the photographer, but let him do his own job. I yielded reluctantly, and I'm sorry now that I did, for the pictures did not come out. Underlighted, they said. I could have told him that.

On our way home Cornelia remembered that an actor she knew had telephoned her, and was coming up to see her before dinner, so she thought she had better get some Scotch. She leaned forward and asked the driver—this time, a man—to stop at the nearest liquor store. He gave her a quick and reproachful look, and then went back to his driving. "Why, honey," he said, "you know I can't do a thing like that. What's the matter with you?"

Cornelia explained meekly that she had not realized there was anything the matter in asking to go to a liquor store.

Our chauffeur rebuked her. "There's plenty. It isn't allowed. I can go get you somewhere and I can take you some place else, but I can't stop between for any pleasure like a liquor store."

So we got out, abashed, a few blocks from home, and trudged to the nearest liquor store. The food markets along the way were irresistible—bins spilling over with fat oranges and grapefruit, avocados, green vegetables, crisper and greener than those I had left in the East. I could not resist them, so I suggested to Cornelia that I cook dinner for us that night, and she was highly receptive to the idea.

While she went in for her Scotch, I marketed happily. Looking for Postum—and not finding it—I wavered among the many brands of California cereals and fruit beverages. But "Hollywood Cup" was my final selection. It seemed to have an air of the cinema about it. The varieties of tedious and tasteless Melba toast were wide, too. Melba toast from lima beans, from soya beans, probably from alfalfa, too. It seemed to me that something out of practically every field in California had been pressed down into Melba toast. But at the meat counter there was no variety whatever; in fact, there was no meat. I had seen cartoons of what the meat counters were likely to look like, but this real one was literally and actually empty. I asked the butcher one of those silly questions which women, more than men, seem prone to ask in the face of the obvious. "Haven't you really any meat at all?"

The butcher looked furtively up and down the counter,

and seeing no one standing near me, leaned over close to my ear and whispered, "I could let you have two lamb chops."

"Isn't it all right for me to have them?" I whispered back anxiously. This was before rationing.

"Sure," he said. He evidently had asthma and his voice creaked like a rusty gate. "Only I can't display the little amount of meat I got. It only makes my customers want more, and then I can't satisfy 'em. See?"

I did not, very clearly, but I gratefully took the two lamb chops which he wrapped up in a back room, and handed to me around the end of the counter.

We ate that night baked potatoes from Idaho, celery from Utah, artichokes from California; and we drank Mexican beer. But the lamb chops were jewels imported from the East.

I GRATEFULLY TOOK THE TWO LAMB CHOPS WHICH HE
WRAPPED UP IN A BACK ROOM, AND HANDED TO ME
AROUND THE END OF THE COUNTER.

Chapter Five

Sheridan Gibney telephoned us one morning to ask if we would like to come down to his office, which was on the third floor, for a little round of collaboration. Cornelia and I had been, we thought, collaborating like all get out, but we were pleased and a trifle apprehensive. It was like being asked by the principal to come to his office. We found him leaning back in his desk chair to an almost horizontal position, but he kicked with his feet, jerked his head back and forth a few times a little in the manner of an East Indian dancer until the balance of the chair changed and brought him back to an upright position with a bang and a jar. Then he smiled at us both in modest pride.

"This is Rose," he said, and pointed to his secretary, who grinned at us and at him indulgently.

Our principal must be over twenty-one years old but he does not look it. He has a wife and three children, and furthermore he was in Paris the same summer that Cornelia and I were, and was, at that time, an undergraduate at Amherst. Therefore, unless he is like one of the little boys or girls you read about who come from obscure places in South America or India and display a startling precocity, he is a contemporary of Cornelia's and mine. His face and hair are brown, his eyes blue, and they all buckle up like an accordion when he laughs. He cries, too, when he laughs, and not a pretty tear, but a handkerchief-soaking freshet that is a joy to all beholders; and he has a solemn and deep pleasure in devices. I am sure he had put some little time and study before Cornelia and I arrived, in seeing how far back he could maneuver his desk chair without its tipping over, and how suddenly, and, with the use of what muscles, snap it into place again.

We sat down in comfortable chairs, Cornelia and I, in front of and at one side of the desk. Rose was seated on a couch. Sheridan expounded to us that the best position for writing was flat on one's back, the feet propped high in the air, the eyes closed. I think he said that when the blood was out of the head the ideas were clearer, or perhaps it was vice versa. I did not try to grasp it because I knew that Cornelia's New England spine would never stretch itself out in any such manner for work, and that I should fall asleep. Cornelia, sitting up very straight at the suggestion of the couch, said that she herself thought better if she chewed gum, and better still if she chewed two sticks at once. In all the years I had known her, I had never seen chewing gum in her possession, but I had also never seen her at work. From this moment on, however, I was to watch daily la soignéed Skinner chewing a ruminative wad of Wrigley. She opened her bag and, in a fine spirit of helping us with our thoughts, passed around a package. I took one, grateful for any mental aid. Rose did not care for any, and Sheridan preferred his pipe.

He pushed his chair back only a little—he had proven how far he could make it go—and began to trace the outline of a pattern for a story from *Our Hearts Were Young and Gay*. We might as well not have bothered about the dialogue we'd been doing, but we did not mention it. He began the story in New York, and I found myself hearing about the girls with the greatest interest. They were strangers, and yet familiar to me, so that presently I felt confident enough about them to interrupt.

Would they, I suggested, have been together at a debutante dance in New York? After all, Emily came from the Middle West, didn't she? As if I didn't know! Wouldn't they have been more likely to be together at a college prom? Sheridan agreed, and turned to Cornelia for her opinion, but she was looking dreamily past us toward the window just chewing, so we did not intrude. "All right, Rose," Sheridan said, "I think we are ready." And he began to dictate. About an hour later Cornelia broke in. By this time we had changed the opening so that Emily was in the infirmary with the measles and Cornelia at a prom. Then we had taken them through a scene of persuading their families to give consent to their going abroad, from there to the meeting on the dock and their embarking, the purchase of a coat for Emily, and a scene in the stateroom.

"I think," Cornelia proposed, "that the dance ought to be in the gymnasium, with the horses and apparatus all around."

We all looked at her, curious. Sheridan said he didn't quite see why they would dance in the gymnasium on board ship. He would think it would have to be either the ballroom or the deck.

"I'm not talking about the ship," Cornelia told us. "What has the ship got to do with it? I'm talking about that opening scene."

We were, we explained, far beyond that now.

"Are you?" she said in surprise. "I didn't hear you."

There was a silence, strained for the rest of us but not for Cornelia.

"I work very slowly," she elucidated kindly, to bring us in touch with her processes, "and alone. I am not at all used to working like this."

I should not have said that it was *my* daily custom to sit in the office of a motion picture producer and dictate a scenario with him. I did not remark this aloud, however, and she went on, "I have a little cabin down on Long Island not far from where we live at St. James. It's quite small, but it's right on the Sound, up on a cliff, and has the most beautiful view." We were pleased that Cornelia had a cabin and a view. "I work there all by myself, and very slowly. In long hand, too." Rose looked apologetically at her brusque shorthand. "So, you see, I haven't got to the ship, but I do think the opening dance ought to be in the Bryn Mawr College gymnasium where the two girls are. I think the stag line ought to be along one side, and one or two of the boys could be part way up the ladders against the wall as if they were looking out from the rigging of a ship. And one boy could have his arms through a pair of rings and be swaying gently, just a little bit tight, so that the chaperons along the other side are watching him with a faint suspicion."

Sheridan and I looked at each other. He concentrated on his pipe a moment or two, and then he said gently, "We'll go back, Rose, to the opening scene."

Cornelia outlined it in greater detail. She told us, too, in greater detail, about her life at the cabin. That was the way the scene was done and, though we did not say so, it was better than our version. Cornelia went back to her window vigil, and her gum.

Sheridan explained to me—and to Cornelia out of courtesy—how important it was to remember the limitations and the advantages of the technique of a movie. For instance, he said, you could not, as you could in a play, jump from one place to another and from one period of time to another without an indication of the intervening places and dates, because you had, after all, no theatre program which could read, "Act II, London, six months later." Therefore you had to bring your characters step by step and day by day to London, or indicate very clearly their destination, and the time of their arrival. Most important of all, you could not, for the sake of comedy or for any other reason, bring in a scene that was irrelevant because the camera emphasized everything so that any little by-path would stand out. Every scene, every character, every speech must be indispensable to the progress of the plot, and the plot must move swiftly. There was no time to spare in a movie, so you must knit tightly and relevantly.

The door opened violently at this moment and banged against the wall. "Come in, Frank," Sheridan said superfluously. "What's the matter?"

Frank told him he would just sit down a minute. He was tall, broad-shouldered, white-haired, and angry red-faced. "How do you do, Miss Skinner and Miss Kimbrough?—I know who you are." He shook himself down on the couch beside Rose and grabbed his hair in both hands. "Those so-and-so's! What do you think they want now?"

We didn't know who wanted what.

"The front office," he stormed. "And I'll tell you *what*. I'm writing about the escape from Bataan and they want a scene slipped in for Dorothy Lamour. Telephoned just fifteen minutes ago. Slip in Dorothy Lamour! I'll slip them something. Got any ideas?" He glared at Cornelia and at me.

Cornelia shook her head.

"She will have one for you in a week or two," I told our visitor, "and it will be good."

The visitor got up again from the couch. "Two weeks! I have to have it now. I'm going to lie down." He stormed out the door and turned back. "My name is Frank Butler. Good-bye."

Sheridan was the first to speak after the door had closed. "You see," he said, "just as I was telling you—every scene must be essential and tightly packed into the plot."

Charlie Brackett joined us at lunch that day in the Commissary. He is respectfully and affectionately conceded to be one of the top writers and producers there. I consider him, too, one of the wittiest men I have ever met. And the wit is not of the sort that, when quoted, must be followed by an apologetic, "It was awfully funny the way he told it." Perhaps I admire his wit, too, because he is so generous with it. I have always heard that playing tennis with a top rank player brings out of you a better game than you know how to play. I cannot vouch for that. Even with Tilden facing me across the net, I think I should still hold the racket with both hands before my face at a coming ball. But to face Charlie Brackett across the table is to make of me a Tilden of a conversationalist. He laughs at what I say, which is, of course, always the most heady stimulant, changes artfully a word or two, until, seeming to repeat them for his own enjoyment, he turns my remarks into glittering phrases and I am, or seem to myself to be, sending out and receiving brilliantly the most spectacular strokes.

But at this moment Charlie was in no mood for strokes of any kind except, perhaps, on the head with a soothing, "There, there." He folded his arms, elbows on the table, and glowered moodily at us. "I'm stuck," he said, "unquestionably, irrevocably stuck. A man has got to buy a house and live in it, and I can't for the life of me think why. Do you know anything about music?" He turned abruptly to me.

"We can do part singing," Cornelia contributed, "without going off."

"Well, then," Charlie wanted to know, "would a man, who is a musician, take this house which is on the ocean because he had perfect pitch and so had the ocean?"

I said dubiously that I thought it was asking a good deal of the ocean.

Charlie was almost irritable. "All right, then, why? Why does he have to take it? The house, it turns out, is haunted. He doesn't know that until later, but he has to want that house more than any other. Now why does he? There's got to be a reason for it that makes any other choice impossible."

Sheridan said across to me that that was what he had been trying to explain about movie writing technique.

"I know," I said, "essential, like Dorothy Lamour."

There seemed to be no way of reconciling the pitch of the ocean to the pitch of the musician, and no way of getting him into the house by means of it. So we let the whole topic go, and I tried to distract Charlie by asking him about the five-letter-word game which his table of writers played every day. He drew a pad out of his pocket on which was stamped the pattern of five squares across and five down. "We had the stamp made," he explained sheepishly. "It saves time." He tore off a sheet for Sheridan and one for me, offering one to Cornelia, too, and she took it. But she was musing, and her mind was not on the game. After the first round she withdrew while we played two or three games more. Then she came suddenly into conversation.

"I have a cabin, down at St. James, Long Island. It's very small but it is directly on the Sound and has a wonderful view. I adore it. There's no particular reason why, but I do. I work. . . ."

"Alone," Sheridan and I said in chorus.

"Yes," said Cornelia, pleased that we should remember. "That's right—I work there all alone. I'm not very good at working with other people and I work very slowly. But it does seem to me that it is perfectly possible to have an indefinable pull toward a certain house or place in which to live, and it has nothing to do with any circumstances. It's reason enough in itself that one does prefer a certain house to another, although the one you discarded may be far more suitable and practical. I think you have to take into consideration the responsiveness of a human being to an environment."

She was working around to the haunted house on the ocean, and in the end she had a psychological reason for the man's purchase of that house and no other. And at the very end, that is, the time at which I am writing this chronicle, she is back in Hollywood, playing a part in Charlie Brackett's motion picture, *The Uninvited*, (from Dorothy MacArdle's book of that name) the plot of which with the aid of her cabin on Long Island she helped develop.

After lunch that day Sheridan walked us back to the office by way of the gymnasium. "I think," he explained, "you ought to meet Jim. He is a great character around here." The gymnasium was a modest, one-story building, painted a dark green. Around the front there were big tubs of palms, and other plants which I did not recognize. I have no idea whether they actually belonged to the gymnasium or whether they were destined for a movie set and had been deposited there only temporarily while

the set itself was being constructed. They stayed, however, as long as I was at Paramount, and were quite
charming, giving the effect to this little spot in the midst
of the towering stages all around, of a nice, cozy frame
house with a front yard. And it turned out that the building was the original one of the Paramount Studios, the
place in which all the first pictures were made. It had
never, perhaps because of sentiment, been torn down.
The rest of the lot had simply been built up around it.
Now it was the gymnasium, presided over by Jim.

He came to the door at Sheridan's knock, dressed in
immaculate white duck trousers, white sneakers, and an
undershirt which provided an unobstructed vision of his
magnificent shoulder and arm muscles. He was very
tanned, of course—I was already beginning to look upon
this as the California State color—and he had brown suède
eyes; they were very small, like little triangles. His hair
was brown, curly, with deep, wide waves, the sort we
used to set with combs. He looked like some one famous,
of whom I have seen pictures, but whom I could not quite
place—"Gentleman Jim" Corbett, I think.

Sheridan introduced us, and Jim in a soft brogue said
he hoped we'd come round to see him, and he would be
glad to take care of us. Before we left, we had made an
appointment to come back that afternoon at half-past
four for a massage, partly because Sheridan and Jim
agreed that it was the best way in the world to take off

weight—and the California food was so good—but even more than that because, we confided to each other afterward, we wanted to be able to come home and say that we had strolled over from work to have a massage on the lot every day.

Back in the office, we started in again with gum, pipe, and Rose. The synopsis moved along, but I found myself confusedly and rapidly entering into a split personality. At one moment we talked about Cornelia and Emily, and they were simply characters in a story. Suddenly we would find ourselves saying "you" and "I," taking an active part, and at the same time discussing ourselves as if we were other people. It was very confusing. Sheridan would say, "Cornelia, I think you leave the dance abruptly when you discover that your safety pocket is hitting against your partner."

"No, I don't think so," Cornelia would answer. "I think I try to get over near Emily to see if she is having the same trouble."

And I would join in. "That's right. I saw you coming toward me, and I knew from the look on your face that something was the matter." We even confused tenses like that so that we talked as if the incidents were happening at the moment and to us, until when Sheridan said, "That concludes the scene, and Emily dissolves to the façade of the Rouen cathedral." I had a definite and confusing sensation of dissolving.

It was no wonder that when we reached the gymnasium at four-thirty I was preoccupied. Jim showed us how to work the shower and get wrapped in the sheet for the massage and then left us until we were ready.

Cornelia had decided that she would take a cabinet bath as well as a massage, to lose more poundage. I had never taken one and did not in the least like the look of it, which made the schedule much easier. I would have a shower and be massaged while Cornelia sat in the cabinet and then rested. Then I could stay on the table and doze off while Cornelia in the other room was massaged—a sequence which suited me perfectly. I pattered around, undressing and turning on the shower, still talking of the scene we had just completed. Cornelia got into the cabinet, sat on the stool provided, and I closed down the boards around her neck as I imagine people used to be locked up in the stocks. Then I went on into the shower which faced the cabinet, talking all the time, and raising my voice above the noise of the water. I had just begun to work out a possible sequence, which had baffled us, when Cornelia started to interrupt me, but I begged her not to say anything or I should lose the thread. If she would just let me finish, she could tell me what she thought of it. She seemed dissatisfied at this, but I could not hear what she said over the noise of the shower, and I went on inexorably, shouting my ideas. When I had finished I called across to her, "What do you think of that? Then you tell me what you've been trying to say."

And she shouted back, "I think it's all right, and I only wanted to say that you have your hat on."

It dried eventually, of course, but the shape was different.

Jim massaged me with a tantalizing rhythm. His fingers moved in a pattern of sound as precise as an orchestra's and as irresistible as Fred Astaire's tapping feet. I said lazily, almost asleep, lying on my stomach, my face pillowed on my arm, that Fred Astaire ought to dance to it. They could make a wonderful scene, I thought, with his massage, and Fred Astaire doing a dance while waiting for his turn.

The next instant I was shaken violently by the shoulder and Jim was bending down to shout excitedly into my ear, "That's a gag, it's a good gag, it's a wonderful gag. You sell it. I can see it all: I'm standing giving a massage and Fred comes in. I tell him I'll be ready in a few minutes and he says O.K. and he sits down to wait. Then he gets up when I start the pounding."

I interrupted to ask if he always massaged the same way.

"Sure," he said. "I don't know what I do. I got a technique. It takes all ten fingers. I do it the same way every time. I didn't know I was playing a tune. But you've made a good gag out of it."

I asked him what a gag was. I'd heard the word for years, but I didn't really know what it meant.

He stepped back from the table. "You don't know what a gag means? It means everything. Why, Emily, a gag is the movies. Look, I'll show you."

He jumped up on the table and reached on top of a cabinet for a long iron bar with a disc at either end, the sort of thing strong men in vaudeville acts use to demonstrate their powers. He could barely reach it with one hand, but he touched it finally with the tips of his fingers and edged it toward him. Then he swung it over the edge, and it bounced on the floor.

"You see," he explained, "I had this made after my own design. It's plywood, but it looks like the real thing, don't it?" I agreed. "Then I had it put up there. Nobody noticed it for a week or more, but I didn't say a word. I was as anxious as hell—*you* know, it might be a flop. But one day Sheridan Gibney is lying here like you, having a massage, and he sees it. 'Can you lift that, Jim?' he says, and I say, 'Sure, I used to do a vaudeville act with it in the old days. I'll show you.' I tell you, my heart was jumping. Then I get up on the chair and reach for it like you saw me do just now, only I make out that it's almost too heavy for me to get out. I heave and heave and I finally slide it over the edge, strainin' until every muscle is bulging out. And then I let it drop as if it was an accident, right over on top of the couch where Sheridan is laying. He gives a yell you could have heard at the other end of the lot and rolls off that couch on to the floor out of the way. It scared the b'-Jesus out of him. It was a good gag. Now d'ya get what I mean?"

I said I thought I did. He had acted out the entire scene of the plywood dumb-bell in vivid pantomime, ending in the corner beside the cowering Sheridan. Now he came back to the table and bent down over me anxiously. "Haven't you worked up any gags in your picture?" he asked.

I said yes, I thought so. Not anything like that, but we hoped we had some funny spots.

He shook his head. "It don't sound like enough to me. You can't do a picture without gags, you know. It's all the writers out here talk about. They come over to me for a treatment and we talk gags all the time, nothing but gags. It worries the hell out of them all the time."

I asked him if he thought up many.

"Oh, sure, a good many. I work 'em out. They take time, though, you know. You can't do 'em in a hurry. I've got a good one," he went on, "for Skinny in there."

That made me start a little, realizing he was referring to Cornelia, dozing serenely in the next room.

"I got a sheet made not long ago," he went on, "and I'm going to try it on her. It looks just like a regular sheet, see, but it's really only half the size. I'll put it on top of a pile on the cabinet, and when she comes out, she reaches for it, of course. She's not thinking anything about it because there are a lot there. So she goes on into the room and gets on the table. Then she tries to put the sheet on it. She's new at this—she hasn't been coming over here very long—and she thinks she just hasn't got the trick of it. If she puts it lengthwise it won't reach over the sides of the table. If she tries it the other way, it won't go down to her knees. You see what a laugh that is?"

I was quite shocked, and I told him he mustn't see her do that—he simply could not go so far.

Jim's eyes became more patent leather than suède. I think he was really angry. "Who said anything about seeing it?" he demanded. "What do you think I am, Emily? I don't like you thinking things like that about me. But, my God," his eyes began to twinkle again, "what a laugh I'm getting, standing out here and picturing her in there, turnin' the sheet this way, tryin' it down that way, not knowin' what the hell's the matter with it. They were hard to get made, you know," he broke off, seriously, "so they'd look just like the other sheets, I mean."

And a week later he did try it on Cornelia, exacting from her afterward a minute description. She had been thinking about something else at the time, she told him, and so she had worked over it patiently, without realizing that anything was wrong. Jim was completely happy. "What a laugh," he kept saying over and over. "I got a good one that time." Not that he laughed himself. He was as nervous as a woman trying out a new recipe and awaiting the verdict of the family on it, but his soul was satisfied. There was a good gag.

This was still another branch of the technique of movie writing, and I learned more about it after that day at Jim's. I learned that gags were so important that pictures were often identified by the ones used in them, but that there were various kinds. When Mervyn Leroy out at Metro-Goldwyn-Mayer said one morning about a book he had been asked to read and consider as a picture, "It's the kind of a book you can put down," his comment was at Paramount not many minutes, I gathered, after he had said it—and at all the other studios, too, I suppose. And it was labeled the best gag so far of the week. A gag, therefore, was a practical joke, a situation, a funny line or a good comeback, except that it was not funny to the person responsible for it. It was valuable. You might sell it, or you might even work a picture around it. You could make a fortune out of it. When such a prospect was within the realm of possibility, no wonder no one in Hollywood could afford to be funny about humor.

A few days after our lesson from Jim, Edgar Bergen discussed the problem with Cornelia. "The unexpected," he said sorrowfully, "is always good for a laugh." Cornelia suggested that her father always used to insist, along with Charlie Chaplin, that the most successful type of humor was that which included arousing the pity of the audience.

I interrupted. That was what we were insisting on for our book. If the audience laughed at the two girls in the picture and at the same time said, "Oh, the poor things, how could they have been so dumb? Wasn't that awful," then it would be really funny. Bergen agreed to that. I was pleased by his endorsement. Since there was certainly nothing original in the principles of humor which I had expounded, I must have presented them with sufficient lugubriousness to have my technique approved.

But it remained for Jim to give us the best demonstration of all. We had been having daily massages for a week. I could not see that he was stemming the advancing tide of my figure, but his massages were very restful, and I was still enjoying the luxury of strolling across the lot to take them. On this particular day Cornelia was in the cabinet and I on the table, Jim doing his finger tap-dancing up and down my spine. Suddenly, just outside the window, a roar louder than all the cannons I ever heard fired off in Muncie on the Fourth of July and Decoration Day combined, belched at us with such vibration that the windows rattled, the table on which I was lying shook under me, and I shook on top of it. My ears felt as if I were going through a tunnel; my teeth jarred until I held my tongue between them; even my spine and its vertebrae quivered. I could not think at all when it happened; but some time afterward—I have no idea how short or how long—the idea penetrated to me that this must be what an earthquake is. At that very instant Jim, his back to me, began frantically turning the knob of the door which led from our room into the gymnasium.

"It's the Japs," he said hoarsely. "I knew they'd get here. It's the Japs."

And simultaneously with that came a rattle like the sound I have heard in the movies to represent a machine-gun. My sheet and I were off the table with a speed which no camera as yet developed could have caught. And the speed was sustained by a new sound, rising above the rattle of the machine-gun, a sort of wild, explosive tattoo, which I identified as what I have read of as "a rain of bullets."

Jim yelled above the uproar, "Where are you going?"

And I had only voice enough to answer, "To Phila-delphia—they won't come to the Atlantic seaboard." I grabbed the handle of the door leading to the outdoors and the east, though I had no idea which way the east lay. The door was locked, and my sweating inability to open it gave Jim time to reach me with a rush.

"You crazy!" he said. "You dope! You can't go out there with a sheet on. What would people think?"

I had no words to tell him my complete indifference to public opinion.

He patted my arm and said slowly and solemnly, "Dearie, it's a gag. It's the best gag that's ever been pulled."

There was a sigh from the adjoining room and the rain

of bullets stopped. The bullets had been Cornelia's feet, encased with her in the cabinet, and beating a wild tattoo of impeded flight with me to Philadelphia. We got her out and on to the table in the adjoining room. I went back to the one I had just left. We lay very quiet, and Jim continued, "You see, they're shooting a bombardment today and they're taking the scene outdoors on that miniature lake. I knew it was coming, but I decided not to say anything."

I opened my eyes and looked across at Cornelia to see if she were all right. I found her looking at me, and we nodded weakly but reassuringly to each other.

"I didn't know how it would develop," Jim continued, "so I thought I'd just wait and see what happened. I knew they was goin' to set the charge off right outside this building, and it would give us a terrible wallop, and I wanted to see what you two girls would do. Well, I saw." He closed his eyes a moment, savoring the full beauty of the recollection. "When you sat up on that table, I could see you thought it was the real thing, whatever it was."

I said I thought it was an earthquake.

"An earthquake! Why, an earthquake don't put on that much of a show. Well, anyway, I saw it had got you, so I acted fast. You saw me trying to get through that door into the gymnasium. Of course, I was just acting," he explained modestly, "but, boy, that was good when I said it

"WHERE ARE YOU GOING?"
AND I HAD ONLY VOICE ENOUGH TO ANSWER, "TO PHILA-
DELPHIA—THEY WON'T COME TO THE ATLANTIC SEA-
BOARD."

was the Japs. And then I had the idea to run my fingers up and down the Venetian blind beside the door. I figured you'd never see me doing it and it sounded just like a machine-gun, didn't it?"

I said yes, it did.

"That was wonderful," Jim reminisced, "when you cut loose across to that door. But you had me scared for a minute. I thought you was goin' to streak right out across the lot with that sheet on. Of course in a picture you'd leave it that way—you cutting across the lot—but I'd of been mortified if you'd really gone out there. I must say," he concluded with awe, "I think this is the best gag I ever dreamed up. If you can use it in your picture," he added a generous postscript, "you're welcome to it, but if you can't, I'll just tell it to some of the boys to see what they make of it."

Cornelia told him in a faint voice that he was welcome to it. And Jim was touching in his gratitude. He went out through the gymnasium, presumably to start telling the boys, and Cornelia and I got dressed. We were still a little shaky, and we had nothing to say. But in the taxi cab going home Cornelia turned to me.

"I don't want to be too unpleasant about it," she said, "but presently, as you think it over, you're going to realize that you were starting out for Philadelphia leaving me trapped in that cabinet."

I was shocked. I had not thought about it until that

moment, but I protested that I would have come back. I would have remembered in just a minute, as soon as I had reconnoitered a little.

Cornelia said nothing.

I asked why she was trapped in the cabinet. She could always get out of it before. No one had ever had to help her.

She looked embarrassed. "Well," she admitted, "I did get confused. You have to put the two flaps up together. I kept pushing at them one at a time, and the one coming up against the one going down has dislocated my neck. I was practically hanging myself."

Some time later we remembered, from a college course, that behavior in a crisis was the real evidence of CHARACTER AND INTELLIGENCE.

Chapter Six

The scenario moved along, and we settled down into a schedule. Every morning we went to our principal's office and worked straight through until lunch time; that is, Sheridan and I worked forward. Cornelia went back. After a little trial spin with her gum, allowing Sheridan and me just time enough to be well into the scene planned for that day, she would tell us about her cabin on Long Island, at St. James, its view, how she worked alone, and how slowly she worked, and that the scene, naming one which we had brought to a close anywhere from twenty-four hours to a week ago, would perhaps go better if . . . And she would outline, apologetically, a treatment which we could not ignore—though not for want of trying. To save face, Sheridan and I would occasionally change a word, but I doubt if Rose paid any attention. She knew when we were outwitted, and she followed Cornelia's dreamy leadership meticulously. Cornelia always removed her gum before she began her suggestions, and we came to know that when she held up the top sheet of the scratch pad on which, most of the time, she drew abstracted abstractions, and dropped her gum into it, folding up the corners and then putting the little packages into the waste-paper basket, we were about to turn back the pages.

Sheridan, too, had "man-working-here" signs which I grew to recognize. When he opened the left-hand top drawer of his desk and began to rummage about, it meant that he was not satisfied with what we had just done, or was stumped about how to proceed. He would eventually find and bring out three boxes of pills, hover over them for several minutes, and finally make a selection, sometimes from only one, sometimes from all three. He was always preoccupied at such times and yet intent on the pills. Suddenly he said one day, "Goodness, I never offered you these. I'm so sorry. Will you have one?"

That gave me the courage to ask him about them. I had been haunted for some time by the speculation over what malady he could have which demanded such a variety and at such irregular intervals, also what were the symptoms which made him know the one or combination to select. I was somewhat at a loss to know exactly how to ask him, and yet determined not to let this opportunity go by. So I said timidly that if he would rather not tell me, I should understand, but I was concerned about the pills and what they were.

Sheridan looked up from a sort of eenie-meenie-minie-mo over them. "They're some left over from my wife's last pregnancy," he said. "And I figured it was more or less the

101

same thing after all—I'm creating, too. And when it isn't going so well, I just try one or two or all of these pills."

I asked if he thought they helped.

He said yes, he thought they did, and was I sure I would not have one or two?

I was sure.

He took one from each box, poured out a glass of water from a trick carafe Rose had given him, and which he enjoyed, a separate glass for each pill, and we went on.

Rose had no outward signs of method, but her method itself was flawless. She never once vouchsafed an opinion, but whenever Sheridan said, "Take that out, Rose, we'll try it another way," she would answer, "I didn't put it down, Mr. Gibney." I never knew her to laugh at a line we three encouraged ourselves was funny, or at a situation. She was a complete master of the Hollywood technique of humor. But her kindliness and her perception were remarkable. On a day when the script was going badly, she always stopped me to ask about my twins at home, and coaxed me into telling some anecdote about them. It made me homesick but it took my mind off the work, which was very smart of her.

We took our minds off our work nearly every day, too, by visiting a set. This was a generally accepted and recommended phase of motion-picture writing technique, and the approved time was immediately after lunch. The only dissenters to this program belonged to the school of taking a nap. Which school the front office preferred I do not know, but in every office which I saw, a couch was provided.

Cornelia and I could almost always be found on the set of *Lady in the Dark*. The first day on which we were formally invited and formally inducted, was the morning after Hedda Hopper's column about us, and was obviously the result of her friendly prodding on our behalf. The wedding scene—the telephone message came—was going to be shot at three o'clock on Monday afternoon, and Mitch (Leisner, the director) would be delighted if we would care to see it. Sheridan took Cornelia and me, and as we came near the stage, he pointed out some trucks lined up outside. Wide squat motors of some sort were pounding and thumping on each of them. "This whole picture is being shot in technicolor," he explained, "and it takes so much current they had to borrow those extra dynamos from other studios." Two or three policemen were guarding them.

Another policeman was guarding the inclined entrance to the stage and would not hear of our passing. "There's nobody gets in to see this," he announced proudly. "That's orders."

I urged Sheridan in a whisper to tell who he was, knowing despondently that it was the last thing in the world he would do. It was, and we turned to go. But a young man came running out after us. He was Mitch's assistant,

103

he told us breathlessly. We were expected and they were waiting for us. I swept past the policeman with triumph.

Inside there was no such gloomy darkness as we had stumbled through to reach the marriage scene in *So Proudly We Hail.* This was a wedding scene too, but there was no darkness and the set was certainly not gloomy. Rising up in the very center in a glare of light was a wedding cake, the size of a house, not a big house, perhaps, but a medium house. It rose in scalloped tiers of icing to a bell on the top, which was not, I suppose, the size of the Liberty Bell at home in Philadelphia, but it looked comparable. The cake seemed to have taken the place of an altar in a church because an aisle stretched away from it carpeted in the typical white that is unrolled just before the bridal procession enters. On either side were the choir stalls, and these were filled with the choristers, about fifty I should think. They were dressed in choir robes which were very full, and of a shade that was not quite gold and not quite green. From the play, *Lady in the Dark,* I recognized that this must be the wedding dream scene, but I only realized some time later that the reason the colors in this scene and the others which I saw were so difficult to define was that they were representing colors as seen in a dream, not sharp, but fuzzy so that you could not quite tell just what they were. I had always heard how extraordinary the movies were in their precision of detail, and I am sure there are more spectacular instances of it

than this, but for me the detail of imagination in this con-
ception of a dream is hard to surpass.

Someone pointed out a scaffolding high overhead, to
which some of the big flood lights were attached, and a
ladder against the wall leading up to it. I shook my head
at that at once. We were speaking very little and very low
because the director was giving last-minute instructions,
but I managed to convey my distaste of almost any height
above floor level. Cornelia and Sheridan, however, walked
over to the wall and began scaling the ladder. They went
up and up until I could not even look. I knew that nothing in the world would have been more foolish than my
going with them because, even had I been able to make it
at all, I should have kept my eyes tightly shut the whole
time I was there, and this would certainly have defeated
my purpose. I finally gathered up my courage and
glanced back and there they were up on the top, sliding
gingerly down to a sitting position on the platform, no
back to it, and nothing to hold on to but the railing,
which, when they were seated, was above their heads.
Cornelia let go with one hand to wave down to me in
what, even from that distance, was plainly discernible as
a very condescending gesture.

At that instant someone tapped me on the shoulder
and whispered that Mitch wanted to know if I would
like to go over and stand beside him while the scene was
shot. I followed my guide and was introduced to Mitch

on the lowest tier of the wedding cake. He was talking to Ginger Rogers when I came up. She was sitting, for a few moments of rest before the taking of the scene, on a high stool, which had been drawn up to the wedding cake altar. Mitch introduced us and I talked with her briefly before I stole another glance far up at the swinging platform. In spite of the distance, I could see quite evidently, and with great satisfaction, that Cornelia's superiority had faded away, and that she was considerably irked to look down from that inaccessible height upon me with Mitch on one side and Ginger on the other.

Ginger was friendly and engaging and utterly without affectation, but absorbed in her job. She listened to Mitch like a little girl learning a lesson word for word from a teacher. She was anxious about the coming scene and very tired, but for all her preoccupation she asked me how we liked being out there, how the work was coming along, and where Cornelia was. When I pointed her out up in the eaves, Ginger marveled and waved at her. Cornelia showed off a little by letting go the railing with both hands to wave back.

Mitch said he thought they were ready to try a rehearsal, and Ginger slid off the stool with the help of three or four people to carry the train of her fabulous wedding dress. He pointed to some trucks drawn up to one side of the stage. "That's where the dry ice is," he explained.

As an explanation it left a good deal to be accounted for. I could not imagine why there was dry ice in the first place. Cornelia always insists that I improvise elaborate explanations for things I do not understand. Perhaps that is so, because the only reason I could conjure up for the dry ice was that ice cream was to be served to accompany the wedding cake, and to a great many people, I imagined, if it required trucks of dry ice. And I presumed dry ice was necessary in the first place to keep the ice cream frozen to a proper mould and consistence for the camera. It turned out to be nothing in the least like that.

Suddenly from a pipe hole, concealed in the lowest tier of the cake directly beside us, came pouring a cloud of steam, and simultaneously other clouds from similar holes around the cake and along the aisle. The peculiarity of the steam was that, instead of rising, it sank in soft, thick folds to the floor, going up to a height of only about three feet or less. And again Mitch repeated the now even more obscure words, "you see, that's the dry ice." At the same time men appeared upon the set carrying hoses with long nozzles and, holding these high above their heads, turned them on to let out other clouds of steam. Only, this steam stayed in the air at the height at which it was directed. "Brett smoke." Mitch pointed to it. "They use it for sky writing." It hung in tremulous clouds and wisps, just a little above our heads.

A whistle blew, the stage was cleared, the signal given,

107

and the procession moved up the aisle. It walked through the clouds on the floor and brushed against those trailing in the air, because it was a dream, and the people were not walking at all, but floating. Long ago when I saw Douglas Fairbanks ride through the air on a carpet, I knew that the movies belonged in the world of magic, and when I saw these people in a dream float toward me through clouds I knew all over again with grown-up conviction that magic *is* the world in which the movies should live.

Just as the procession reached the altar, there was a crash somewhere behind us. It sounded to me like the impact of a body falling from a great height to the floor. My knees turned to jelly, and I did not have the strength to look around. But it was not Cornelia. It was a light which had broken away from its fastening up on the scaffolding and hurtled down, not striking, by a merciful Providence, any of the workmen and actors below. Cornelia said later that when it fell, it had, of course, scared the daylights out of her, and that she had heard herself saying afterward, "That's worse than a sandbag falling in the theatre."

At that, she said, an electrician nearby on the platform stopped what he was doing and came over to her. "Excuse me, miss," he apologized, "but I heard what you said. I can tell you're from the theatre, and so am I. And I bet-cha there's not one of them" (he pointed with contempt to the crowd below) "that would know what a sandbag was." He talked sadly and reminiscently a few minutes more about the theatre, and then went back to his work. But when Cornelia started to descend the ladder, he waved aside another workman who came along the catwalk to help her. "She don't need no help," he assured the newcomer proudly. "She's from the theatre, she is. She knows about the flies. Don't give her a hand." He beamed proudly at Cornelia. "It would be an insult to her."

It would not, Cornelia confided, have been anything of the kind. It had taken her quite some time to get over the giddiness of going up the ladder, and the prospect of looking down and going down, made her very sick at her stomach. Nevertheless, she was filled with pride at such commendation, and it helped her knees, too. Some time later she began to wonder just what the electrician thought her occupation was in the theatre that placed her work up among the flies and sandbags.

As she came toward me, I pretended not to notice her, though I had watched with considerable apprehension on my own part every step of her descent. But I was savoring the exhilaration of being the one for the first time in our long years of friendship to introduce her to a celebrity. The savoring was very short-lived. In the middle of what I had thought was an engrossing conversation, Mitch broke away from me and hurried over. "Miss Skinner," he said, "I've been wanting to meet you ever since I heard you were out here. I thought you hadn't come today, and when Miss Kimbrough pointed you out to me way up there on that catwalk, I could hardly believe it. I certainly hand it to you for nerve."

Cornelia arched and bridled with pleasure, but I experienced a moment of regret that the light had not been a body on the floor, not dead, but temporarily disabled.

"I saw you talking to Ginger," Cornelia suggested, when Mitch was called away.

I confirmed that, and said that she was very sweet. If Cornelia would care to meet her I'd be delighted to introduce them. Cornelia said meekly that she would like it very much.

The group of people standing about hooted. "Meet her!" one of them said. "Why, she's been dying to meet you ever since she heard you were out here. She would have been over here before now if she could walk by herself in that wedding gown.

I should not have minded much, I thought, if the body on the floor had had a little more than a temporary disability.

The respect of the motion picture people for anyone of the actual theatre is akin to reverence, and the respect in which Cornelia is held is more closely akin to awe. She represents, of course, to the motion picture actor everything out of his world—a writer, a producer, a director, and a legitimate actor, not to mention a costume and scenic designer.

Cornelia is not the most modest person I know about her success; she is the most completely unaware of it. When you try to tell her that she has achieved distinction, she thinks you are being sweet and polite. When she sees a word of praise in print about her, she feels that its author is either the victim of a delusion, or has been prompted by a benevolent desire to help his fellow human beings get along. She must have thought that the entire portion of the Hollywood world with which she came in contact was under an epidemic of benevolence.

The whistle blew for another rehearsal, and she moved over eagerly to watch it with me from the base level of the wedding cake, and with no inclination for another flight. The whistle blew again, and the clouds from the dry ice poured out through the pipe. The first time I had been aware only of the entire kaleidoscope, and not conscious of anything but general confusion of sight and sound and smell. But now I was acutely aware of the smell that came with the vapor, a sweetish, overpowering odor, and I must have shown it for Mitch took my arm and drew me back out of its direct range. "That can knock you out," he said, and went on to tell us that the day before, which was the first time they had tried it, he had found that this dry ice steam made all the dresses stretch, particularly Ginger's because of its yards and yards of tulle. The dress had, he said, stretched about six inches, so he went over with a pair of scissors to cut it back to its original length. He got down on the floor and lifted up the folds to start cutting, and was almost overcome by the fumes accumulated underneath as she had walked up the aisle. He had to get out in the fresh air as quickly as possible, and Ginger herself had suddenly been overcome on the steps of the cake and been rushed outside and revived. "Of course," Mitch interpolated in apology for such weakness, "she'd been rehearsing since nine o'clock in the morning, and had soaked up an awful lot of the stuff."

I asked if he really meant that they had done this all the day before.

"We did," he answered. "and I don't see a chance of any takes today."

I wanted to know what was holding them up and he shrugged his shoulders, looking at me pityingly. "What always holds you up in pictures?" he demanded. "The camera man didn't get what he wants. I don't mean that he actually took a shot either. I mean just looking, he didn't find it. They find flaws instead. A light is wrong; or a costume's got a bad fold in it; then the angle of the camera isn't right; and, of course, all this is before you add the lines. Somebody blows up in his lines or the sound mixture isn't right. It's a beautiful business, Miss Kimbrough, to stay out of."

112

Chapter Seven

I am not sure that my technical vocabulary is correct. I did my best to learn as many of the words as possible because it gave me satisfaction to be able to use them, and, I thought, it lent a certain prestige. From the looks on the faces of those to whom I was speaking I am not sure that I always used the words correctly. But even if I were not sure, though I tossed them about carelessly, what such phrases as "an establishing shot," a "close cutting shot," "the camera pans," or a "dissolve" might mean, there was something about Mitch's complaint that had an old, old ring of familiarity about it. It bothered me all the rest of that day, like a tune you cannot quite identify, and it was not until several days later that I got it. It came to me in a flash when we were standing watching another scene in another picture.

Just as the director decided he was ready to shoot, the camera man announced that he was not getting the proper angle. If the character who was to be photographed, provided it, he would have to walk off into space, landing in an eight-foot deep canal which had, somehow, within the last twenty-four hours, been run up in the stage. I suppose, technically, *on* the stage is correct, but when the stage is a warehouse of a building, approximating in size the Furniture Mart in Chicago, it seems somehow difficult to speak of being *on* it. One is so much more apt to be in it and lost there. However, the character, to satisfy the camera man, would have had to walk past him and into the canal. But the camera man won. Only, instead of stepping into the canal, the character was provided with a platform built to sustain him after he had passed the camera. The construction of this platform, of course, halted all further work for the rest of the day, and when it was completed and the scene rehearsed, and perhaps eventually the shot taken, the result would probably occupy not much more than a split second of time in the picture, or perhaps not be used at all. Suddenly it all came back to me—the old familiar tune.

I learned it when I was an editor some time ago, but the tune had not changed. I learned it when I sat at a printer's at three o'clock in the morning trying to give a final O.K. for the magazine to be put on the press. And the art director said, "No, I'm sorry. I'm not happy about that cut. There's no use fussing with it any more. I'll have to have a new drawing made."

It is the old war between the art and the editorial departments. And this haunting melody is its battle cry. Once I remembered the tune and the words that went with it, all the strangeness of Hollywood, that is, Holly-

114

wood at work, dropped away and I was out on my own home ground again. There seemed to me to be only one difference.

There was always an hour, however long it had taken to reach, when I, as an editor, could say, "That's enough. We're going to press." And, though the art department moaned for just one more proof to be pulled, with a type block moved a hair's breadth to the right or left, or another photograph be taken because the angle of a book on the table as against the cigarette box was such a jarring line—I could still say, "No. We're not going to change another single thing. Every page is going in the lock-up. The baby has gone to press." And I could say that because, by God's grace, the editor in a publication is the boss.

But there does not seem to be any editor in pictures, at least not any editor-in-chief—the man or woman who can say, "That's enough; this baby is going to press." The executives from the front office come out once in a while and make threats, using as weapons pages of figures and the cost being run up. But they look to be timid folk, who are easily run back to cover. Of course, the hiring and firing come from them, but no one appears bothered by it. They play much more of a game of "Run, sheepie, run" than "Cops and robbers." A robber, however, would be a monumental understatement of an executive's description of a director.

It is true that I never knew one of its business executives to direct the editorial policy of a publication, except under unusual circumstances, but in the editorial department itself there is a chief editor who has the power to say "Go" and "Stop." And when he says "Stop," the food editor cannot have any more cakes made and pictures taken of them. The fashion editor cannot substitute some other drawing which has just come in and for which cuts could be made in a few days more. The homemaking editor has to let the crocheting design stand. And all the other department editors have to turn their pages in, however rank they feel their odor is and how much sweeter they could be made, given only a few days more.

One could be more tolerant about the fussing and fretting over perfectionizing each page if it were done for the greater enjoyment of the reader. But, I maintain, it is not. It is done so that the corresponding editor on a like periodical will have his eye knocked out. Magazines are not issued primarily, I push myself further on a limb by declaring, for the enjoyment of their readers, but for the confounding and confusing of the other magazines in their field. And I heard enough conversation on the lot to think that motion pictures are like them in this, too.

I have, at this point, an uneasy recollection of a small cousin of mine who visited Washington and, after riding from the railway station to the hotel in a closed taxi completely surrounded with luggage piled above his head, went to the writing room and penned a composition entitled, "My Impressions of Washington." I spent just five weeks in Hollywood. And yet I cannot resist, with apologies, going on to the end of the tune.

Jack, or whoever it is at Paramount, is working to show Bill at Metro and the boys at the other studios, what new stunt he can pull. He is not presenting a picture to the public; he is presenting it, with a yah-yah, to his rivals— just as *The Ladies' Home Journal* is issued for *Good Housekeeping, Harper's Bazaar* for *Vogue,* and vice versa. Perhaps that is what makes a picture—or a magazine— good, quite incidentally, for the rest of us, but it is also one of the things, I think, that makes it expensive and long in the doing.

My respect, however, for Jack at Paramount, and George, whatever their names, and every workman there, is humble and deep. They are all specialists. The man, for instance, who runs the crane which holds the camera and camera man, is one of these. From the base of that contrivance, which looks like a yawning dinosaur, he controls the approach and aim of the camera, stopping it at a suspended second so that the camera man can get the exact range specified. The carpenters are equally master craftsmen and artists. I have watched them at work on the impossible. One day, doing the scenario in Sheridan's office, we saw four or five of them outside the window. Since the office is on the third floor, their appearance was odd. We stopped work at once, of course, to investigate, and found

117

that they were putting up a scaffolding for a scene from *China*. The stage, the camera man had decided, was not giving him enough scope. (It would, I thought, have given enough for a chariot race.) So the big doors at the side of the stage were opened—actually a whole wall—the set extended across the road between—with just a footpath left —and three stories up the side of the building, ours, which was opposite. When we left for home that night, the whole structure was shrouded in black canvas like the mourning streamers we had seen in our first view of Paramount on the Cecil de Mille set.

We peeked under the canvas the moment we arrived the next morning—it was like getting under the tent on the lot down by the C. & O. depot in Muncie when the circus was unloading. I hadn't done that since I was twelve, but I don't believe I gaped any more then than I did at this sight of a thick jungle rising up to Sheridan's office windows with live trees, dense underbrush, tropical vines, and through the center of the wilderness a dusty road—at the moment a wagon rumbling over it. The next day, we came around that side of the building to see the set again, and looked down a bare driveway. The jungle was gone, the black canvas and the scaffolding down, and carted away, the wall of the stage closed up again, and Sheridan's windows three stories up serenely restored to view. Sometime, when our backs were turned, they had shot the scene, and the truck-loads of giant trees, underbrush, and dirt road had been carted away. They were finished with the jungle.

I walked through the lobby of the run-down English hotel in *Five Graves to Cairo,* and went close enough to the newspaper rack to see that the flyspecked papers on its rollers were old copies of the London *Times* and the *Daily News.* I climbed a sagging flight of stairs and looked down from the gallery on the court below, with dusty gray palms in the corners, and sand underfoot. Part of the railing hung down over the court, evidently struck and splintered by a bomb. The bedrooms opened off the gallery. The mosquito netting over the brass beds was soggy and dirty, the mattresses were sway-backed, and there was sand everywhere—not enough to be soft underfoot, but gritty wherever I stepped or whatever I touched.

There were imagination and flawless construction. And when the set was lighted, the blinding sun and the dark, musty corners were so sensitively done that I wondered if the electricians were the top specialists of all. But that may have been because I couldn't even grasp what the specialists in the laboratory building were doing, working on the perfecting of sound reproduction, lighting, effect of atmosphere, colors, fabrics, film.

I saw the costume department headed by Edith Head, and she is a genius, with great charm—and humor besides. She can be authentic in period to a fanatic detail, and original at the very same moment.

I could index the department heads and staffs in detail, to read like the faculty list of a university, and with just as eminent qualifications in their fields. And though there is nothing to which I pay quite the same homage as I give to an academic procession, gowned and hooded, I have very nearly the same reverence for these Hollywood specialists.

But, as long as I am giving myself the immense satisfaction of setting forth what Charlie Brackett would term "mighty" strong opinions about the technique of picture making, I see no particular reason to limit myself. There is another practice which I do not understand; or, rather, it is the lack of practice which bewilders me. I was told that a particular scene was to be taken one day immediately after lunch, and I went over to watch it. The scene involved some seventy-five extras besides the principals, and they were all there waiting in costume and make-up. This time the cameras were right; the lights were right; everything was ready to shoot. Two heralds were to introduce the scene, and they took their places on either side of a large doorway. The director explained that from the loud speaker would come a voice counting one, two, three—to eight. On the count eight, the music would start and the heralds were to turn simultaneously, march toward the center of the doorway, meet there, raise their trumpets, blow, separate, and return to their places, keeping time to the music. The eight counts were sounded out;

the music began; so did one herald, but not the other. They tried it again. This time the herald was late. The third time he began on time, but not on the beat. At half-past two I went back to work. The heralds were still rehearsing, the rest of the cast waiting on the other side of the doorway. At half past five, some one passing underneath called up to me, and I put my head out my office window. "I thought you might like to know," he said, "that they've just stopped rehearsing the heralds. They've decided that they can't ever teach that one to keep time, and they're going to get somebody else for the part."

I find myself still wondering why some one did not try out that little scene before all the cast was assembled and the complicated and cumbersome machinery of production under way. It would seem to my untutored mind that when the man was selected to play the part of the herald he might have been asked to walk across the stage in time to music.

I saw Louise Rainer rehearse for one hour a two-minute telephone call. And then Cornelia said in an undertone, "I don't quite see how she could hear with the telephone held against the turban that comes down over her ear." And the director heard her. No one had thought of that, but it involved either rearranging the turban, designing a new one, or planning the whole set the other way around so that the exposed ear would be in the right place. A less important detail seemed to be the fact that Miss

Rainer had not been given her lines for that scene until five minutes before she went on for what was planned as a "take." Therefore she kept missing them. It seems to me that perhaps a rehearsal and an editor out there might come in quite handy.

The reason I saw so many of these scenes being taken was that we were completely bogged down in our own job. You could not, Sheridan had insisted, introduce anything irrelevant to the plot, whatever charm or comedy it might have. And I was determined to introduce a scene from our book which took place in the maze at Hampton Court. I pointed out that the maze was an unusual and charming setting and I should like to see it used. Sheridan answered gently that he, too, would be delighted to see it used if I could provide a reason. So I wrote down reasons, and tore them up, and talked to the writers at lunch— those not absorbed in the word game. And then I roamed about, watching these other pictures. Cornelia was ruminating over a scene we had finished five days before, so there was no attracting her attention. I was alone, balked, and unable to emerge from my dull-wittedness. It may have given me a jaundiced point of view.

It might possibly be true, too, that my impression of the remoteness of executive authority was somewhat colored by the fact that up to the third week no one of them had sufficiently asserted himself to give Cornelia or me a salary check. Or so we thought. "Our checks will be delivered by hand," Cornelia had explained during the first week. "That is the way it is done in the theatre—'The ghost walks'—you know." She repeated it to the girl at the fourth-floor desk. "What day does the ghost walk here?" she asked, with a tinkling laugh of nonchalance, as if that were only her way of passing the time of day.

"Thursday," the girl told her, and we counted the days. But on Thursday, although we left our office only for a quick lunch, no ghost came our way.

She tried again the next day, repeating the question to Sheridan Gibney at lunch. "Thursday," Sheridan told her. But he did not add, "Didn't you get yours?" So, talking it over between ourselves later, we decided that the executives evidently counted from the day on which we arrived, and in our case it was Sunday. Therefore we would expect nothing until Monday. We did not expect anything until Monday, but we did not get anything on Monday either. Nor on the following Monday. Cornelia was smoldering by this time, but I had become shy. I cannot imagine why I turned such a sissy. I am certainly not in the habit of going faint about a discussion of pay, unless it is from over-eagerness or anxiety. But with such lavishness all around and such emphasis on the artistic, it seemed to me greedy and crass to talk about a salary, even if you called it a ghost.

By the third week, however, Cornelia was threatening to report the entire industry to the Actors' Equity. "I am a vice-president," she asserted, "and I've never had very much to do before, but here is something. And I'm going to do it."

Finally she compromised and mentioned it to Sheridan instead. He was appalled.

"What do you mean, you haven't been paid? Did you ask?" he demanded.

No, we admitted, we had not mentioned it up until now.

"Well, what," he insisted, "did the man tell you when you went for it?"

"Went for what?" we asked.

"Your salary."

And then we learned that the ghost did not walk to you, but that you went to a little window in the front of the Paramount office building, like a booth for selling Defense stamps, just beside the entrance on the sidewalk. And that there on Thursday you collected your pay check and signed for it. You could, however, collect it on any other day. And we were on our way before Sheridan had finished explaining this.

Perhaps it was as simple as that for all the other people at Paramount Studios, and it may be that we walked in an aura of complications. But when we presented ourselves at the window, the clerk or paymaster, recognizing us at once, and demanding why in the world we had not been round to see him before, pushed under the wire a check made out to Cornelia Otis Skinner and Emily Kimbrough.

If we were not the Katzenjammer kids, we were, as far as Paramount was concerned, the Siamese twins. We went back to our office to talk it over, and Cornelia made me carry the check in my bag. She was so outraged by this last indignity that she would not so much as hold it.

We are neither of us mathematical giants. Our grasp of the financial structure of the world is of the flimsiest, and this rocked it. If Cornelia deposited it in her account in New York, did we both sign it and mark it to be deposited to her account? Or should we have to go to a local bank and cash it, then ask the bank to give us each a check for half the amount and then be able to deposit it individually? Or should we have to open a joint banking account in Hollywood, deposit the check in it, and then draw out the sum by our own checks? Cornelia by this time was in the kind of tearful rage which demanded she do something "just to show them." What she did was telephone her husband in New York to ask him how we could work out of this. But inasmuch as she lost her nerve about charging it to the company, and her husband was out anyway, it did not show the Paramount executives or us anything. It shook us both, however—the wildness of such a move as a telephone call to New York in the middle of the day.

I was the one who thought of seeing Mr. Dozier. He had wanted us, I reminded Cornelia, to let him know if there were anything he could do. She had objected to my asking him to get us a taxi. Very well, here was something worth his calibre. We went downstairs at once and asked to see him. He was not there, but his assistant, the same one who had made us feel at home on the first day, said she thought perhaps she could take care of whatever we wanted. So we put the whole problem in her lap. The legal department, she told us, was what we needed. And we were in and out of the care of the business executives in less than five minutes.

We never saw a legal executive, either. We only talked to the secretaries. They, after we had explained icily the mistake which had been made—feeling such fools at being shorn of any individuality whatsoever—produced and showed us more icily the contract which we had signed. "Cornelia Otis Skinner *and* Emily Kimbrough," they read.

"Why, certainly," we said, "we wrote the book together. One of us has not signed anything for the other."

No, their spokesman explained, of course one of us would not sign something for the other. That would be illegal. But we did not each sign a separate contract. We both signed one contract. Therefore we would receive one check made out to both, and signed by both.

"And then," Cornelia asked, "what do we do with it? Carry it between us like a banner?"

That froze them up completely. And Cornelia and I swept out.

126

Five days later the legal department called, that is, a secretary in the legal department called, to say that with a great deal of trouble but in answer to our request, separate checks would be issued, and papers to that effect were on their way to our office for us to sign. We signed fourteen papers, and I even took mine into my own office for the operation so that no one could say we had so much as used the same pen. Two days later another secretary from the legal department told us that the separate checks had been put through and might be collected. Somewhere, back in a grotto, an executive had permitted the operation to cut us apart again, but he never came out into the open and acknowledged it. There was no reason why he should have come out for us, but the fact that he did not may have colored my impression about where executives take their stand on a production.

Chapter Eight

During the first week, we came home every night bowed down over the bundles of reading matter furnished us by the research department. It was my fault, Cornelia insisted, because I was so literal with the people who asked if they could do anything for us. When the head of the research department called, I was pleased, I must admit, at the telephone's ringing, and touched by their desire to help. I quickly thought up something for them to do. We had been wondering, I said, how we could put our hands on books and periodicals which would give us the idiom of the period of *Our Hearts*. Cornelia was muttering crossly that she could think of nothing she had done as little wondering about. The research department, however, was tremulously delighted to help, and three hand trucks were required to bring the help to our office.

There were two years, complete, of *The Saturday Evening Post*, *The Woman's Home Companion*, the *Delineator*, *Good Housekeeping*, *Judge*, and *Life*; albums of photographs of early motion picture stars, Rouen, and Paris; books by Scott Fitzgerald, Cyril Hume, and half a dozen or so unknowns; two books on the architecture of

Hampton Court and description of the maze; and three volumes of popular songs and the musical comedies of the twenties. I thought we ought to take them since the research department had gone to such trouble, and it also made me feel young and conscientious again to be carrying home work. Cornelia said it made her feel shabby and senile, lugging bales of old magazines.

After dinner we read as much as we could, though we were always sleepy, and wrote down the words, phrases, and songs which we thought we could use. We spent our evenings in this simple, homely way, partly because the opportunity for any other sort had not presented itself, and partly because the Hollywood climate had at first produced a lassitude above which we could not rise.

But at the end of a week, we were acclimated to the air, and tired of waiting for opportunity. We went to see Nina Koshetz. The world of music knows her as a great singer and an artist of taste and musicianship. But Hollywood knows her, too, as a great teacher of music. And I have known her many years as a friend. She weighs three hundred pounds, but it is her robustness of humor and vitality which cause her to dominate any group of people in any setting, although the three hundred pounds undoubtedly contribute.

She only recently discovered her actual weight, and that by the happy fortune, she says, of going for a drive in the country with her husband and passing a scale on which hay was measured. Previously, she explained, she had broken three scales, and weighing had become too extravagant. But her husband told her surely they could not damage this piece of mechanism, and she felt that she could trust herself to it. So they drove up to the farm house, asked the owner if they might have the use of his scales, returned, and, with the farmer and his family standing in a circle of astonished verification, she stepped majestically on the platform and wrote down the marking in a notebook—three hundred and four pounds. "So you see," Nina boasts, "I do not exaggerate. People say I tell stories. That is not so. I am like a scientist: I have it here in figures, and the farmer will tell you, too."

I do not doubt that the farmer has told it already to as wide a circle as his acquaintanceship includes.

Nina, overflowing a massive, throne-like chair at one end of the long studio-living room, received us with love and calumny.

How wonderful that we were there. How disagreeable of us that we should not have let her know before this. That was not friendly. No. She must give a party for us at once with lots of music, but of course we had been to so many parties and met so many people that was why we had not let her know we were there. So we would not, of course, be interested in her poor party. But she would have one entirely Russian. Russian food, gypsy songs, a really good party. And any of her friends could tell us that she could give them. Only we were not her friends, of course, or we should have stayed with her all the time in Hollywood. And she would have met us at the train. And we should have been so happy all together down at her little house on the beach at Laguna. Only the balcony was all washed away last week. And she was in such despair. If we would believe her, she had cried for two hours the night before without stopping. And when her husband had said, "Thank God, it was not you that went with the balcony," she had sent him out of the room, that he should be so unfeeling. But now God had sent us to her to take the place of the balcony. And it was wonderful because God knew that she adored us both.

We could not hear all of this—although it was not hard to follow the general trend—because two dogs were making such a noise. Marsyk, the white poodle (of sorts), I remembered. "He must be about fifteen years old," I shouted. And Nina corroborated it proudly. It also diverted her momentarily from the welcoming tirade to us, and allowed us to sit down near the throne while she continued. The reason for Marsyk's old age and strength was because he had always been fed Russian food. Caviar, if they had it, beef stroganov because at this house it was wonderful, and of course special food on special feast days. And that was why he was so beautiful and so strong at such an age and could make so much noise. She had told this to the "veter-inerary" to whom she had taken

Marsyk only for him to see what a beautiful, fine dog he was. And he had said certainly it was a fine, beautiful animal, and so she would tell us exactly how to feed dogs to make them like hers. The other dog—I could not hear what she said its name was, but the predominating strain of its family I should say was a Shetland Sheep, was being fed, she told us, along the same principles as Marsyk and had the same remarkable vitality. I saw no reason to doubt it.

A lovely looking young girl came into the room and I realized that this was Margo, the actress. She went straight to Nina on the throne, kissed her without saying a word, and then snapped her fingers, clapped her hands at the dogs and cajoled them through the door evidently into the garden. She turned back, smiling at Cornelia and me —I had thought she had not even seen us, but she explained that habitués of the house always put out the dogs before speaking, to save the voice—and Nina introduced her. I told her I thought her technique with the dogs was superb. She said that all Nina's pupils learned it. "It becomes part of your singing technique, too," she explained. "You are taking a lesson with Nina and learning about breathing. In the middle of it she says, 'Darling, take the dogs into the garden, will you please, and hold that?' And so you hold the breath she has taught you to take, and you lead the dogs across to the garden door and let them out. Then you come back, take another breath as

Nina shows you, and she says, 'Darling, the dogs are barking more outside. Will you please let them in?' And so you hold that breath, and go back to the garden door and coax them in again, past Nina, and out the door to the other part of the house. This goes on back and forth, back and forth, through the lesson, and you think nothing of it. But when you go to a manager for a try-out he says 'Why do you walk up and down the floor, opening doors, and snapping your fingers while you sing?' And you tell him that is the way you breathe."

Nina broke in. "None of my pupils can breathe any more. I have no more men. They are all in the army or the navy or in factories at terrible hours. And the women are pregnant. All of them," she repeated, sonorously, "womiting when I tell them to breathe. Why do you not study with me?" she challenged the three of us.

I withdrew nervously from the exacting demands of singing or pregnancy, and told her hastily that I was working much too hard to take on anything as absorbing as I knew studying with her would be. Cornelia said she would like to study with her if she were in Hollywood again with more time.*

* Editor's note: And while she is in Hollywood as I write this—playing in *The Uninvited*, she is taking lessons from Nina. "A brilliant teacher," she writes. "—marvelous for voice placing. I think she could even have made ι singer of me.

"But Marsyk is dead. She doesn't know of what, although she has taken him to everyone, including a chiropractor. She has a faint doubt that it might be something 'special he ate on Russian Easter'—jewel-encrusted eggs, maybe. Nina is heartbreaking to see, she adored him so."

Nina did not press the point. It had only been a little perfunctory bid for business which she had not wanted to pass up. Did I, she demanded, drink V-8?

I rallied as quickly as possible to the new subject and said that I did. It was the only way, Nina declared, to support the California climate. She gave us a detailed intestinal synopsis of how this support was accomplished, and from there it was but a step to her social activities. We must discuss, she pronounced, the party which she would give for us. Margo, too, had recently returned to Hollywood from New York, and the party must also be for her. Nina described the party at considerable length and enjoyment.

We managed, somehow, to get in a word or two with Margo about the part she was in Hollywood to play; and, very quietly, under Nina's oratory, we talked a little with a Russian friend of Nina's who seemed to be living in the house. When she had actually come into the room where we were, I do not know—some time during the tumult of the dogs, I imagine. At any rate, I had heard about her before. She was Zoia, the original Katinka in the Chauve-Souris when it came to New York. Now I found that she was doing character parts in pictures and enjoying a run of very good luck, because, with the increase in war movies, accents were in great demand. They used her, she said, and all the Russians for any kind of an accent—German, Swedish, Polish—they were getting lots of engagements. The directors, she said happily, were also not quite sure how much of an accent they wanted, and that was another piece of good luck because it meant lots of rehearsals and re-takes, all of which paid.

Nina's husband Garry, she explained, who was away that night at a class in mechanical drawing (Nina had told us earlier, with a certain lack of clarity, that Garry was drawing pictures every night to get into the army), had just finished the part of a German general in Norway. It had lasted a great deal longer than he had hoped for, because at the beginning the director had instructed him to use a heavy guttural accent. Then, becoming alarmed about it as the picture went on, he had faded it out more and more until in the last scene the general was saying, "I say, old thing, will you give me a hand with my boots?" after that, the earlier part of the picture had to be re-taken to match up with it. I felt that this was not perhaps strictly accurate, but at any rate they all felt very jubilant about the war situation in the movies.

Nina brought her outline of the party to a triumphant close, and Cornelia and I got up to leave. It took a long time, of course, and before we were finally away, Nina had pressed into my hand two large cans of V-8.

Three or four days later she telephoned me. The party, she said—the one that she had mentioned the other night —did I remember? (I said I did) had now been taken over by one of her pupils. It would not be so good, of course, but then the pupil had wanted it so much it would be cruel to refuse her; and she would of course run it and say who should be there. And so what did I think of it? And she embarked upon a long list of names, none of which, except for Arthur Hornblow, I had ever heard before. Would they be congenial? Would they be the people we should most like to have? I assured her that they were just the people we should have chosen. She interrupted me abruptly, "Darling, do you like the Jews?"

I was really angry. It happens to be a topic about which I feel strongly. "How can you ask me such a thing?" I said, and I have the impression that I was shouting. What were we fighting for, I asked her. How could she, of all people, ask that. An artist, to be so limited! What did *she* think of some of the greatest artists and scholars in the world? I went on, that I was sorry to be so angry, but that I felt strongly about it these days, cared so much about them anyway, thought it was ignorant to lump them together under a heading *Jews*, and so frightened at the harm that just such talk as hers could do, that I couldn't take it calmly.

There was a long pause. I had time to realize that I had been outspoken and rude, and that Nina was one who could find offense without half trying. Then she answered me quietly, but with mounting fury. "You are crazy," she pronounced judicially. Then she swelled into full voice. "You talk to me about artists and friends,—*me—me* a great artist, and I know it—that it is dangerous in the war—and something I am doing—and *what* am I doing? I am asking you how you like the V-8 joos."

It was not easy to restore her equanimity.

The party itself was very gay, in an exquisite jewel-box of a house, filled with mounds of jade as if the owner had not wasted her time over pieces equivalent to a rib chop, but had bought it on the hoof. And the food was lavish; its seasoning took away one's breath, too. We served ourselves. Arthur Hornblow's was the only house in Hollywood where I saw a servant.

After dinner I found myself in a group of six or eight. The talk had to do with what quality one was attracted to in a man or a woman. I had not known Cornelia was even there until I heard her say, "Emily thinks a man is attractive if he quotes Shakespeare or something—intellectual." That nettled me and I retorted, that she could be taken with a man by the look of him, and it was of secondary importance to her to discover whether he had the power of speech at all or not. When Cornelia's angry roar of protest over this had died down, there was a silence for a moment and into it came the dreamy voice of one of the other guests. "I was attracted," she said, "by his hands, when I married a Turk."

I think I was the only one in the group more interested in her having been married to a Turk than having been first attracted by his hands. Cornelia, I feel sure, would

137

have been interested, but she was backing and filling with pleasure over the whispered asides of one of the men who was analyzing point by point what he found attractive in *her*. I tried to bring the subject back again, but it is a difficult topic to lead into. And then suddenly Nina was at the piano singing, and we were all under the spell of her rich, tender, overwhelming voice.

By the time we left the party, I was still ignorant of the Turkish situation, and, for that matter, of the nationality of three quarters of the people there. I told Cornelia fretfully that I didn't believe anyone in Hollywood knew what nationality or race anyone else came from.

By the time Marian Anderson gave a concert in Los Angeles, our temperature socially had risen. It was certainly not feverish enough to cause anyone anxiety, but at least it was up from the sub-normal torpor of the first week. I thought, then, that out of this improved condition I would round up enough people to give a party.

I have an uneasy feeling that there are certain things in my life about which I am inclined to be boastful; at least I like to bring them into the conversation. I made quite a large collection of butterflies when I was a child; I acted in the Greek plays with Margaret Anglin; I got the lowest mark in mathematics of anyone ever admitted to Bryn Mawr; I have twins; and Marian Anderson is a friend of mine. I consider her the greatest singer in the world, although my opinion may be clouded by my response to her singing, which is as automatic and involuntary as the responsive jerk of a leg to a crack below the knee cap. I weep when Marian sings. Therefore, I know, I am not in possession of all my critical faculties. But in my estimate of the qualities of friendship I feel neither ignorant nor emotionally clouded, and I can say with authority and conviction that she is a lovely, humorous, warm, sensitive human being.

Cornelia leapt at the idea of the party. We began at once to make up a list of people to invite. It was not difficult. All we had to do was to set down the list of the people whom we had met in Hollywood. We went into none of the finer points of who would be congenial with whom. We could not risk weeding out.

I called the desk downstairs and told the manager about the party, for whom we were giving it, and for how many people. He would be delighted, he said, to provide everything we needed, and added that it was nice, he thought, for us to be entertaining such a distinguished artist, too. The people whom we invited evidently agreed with him. I have never known guests to accept so enthusiastically. And I think they were not disappointed.

Marian came with us from the concert. Cornelia and I were in too sodden and nasally blocked a condition to be very adequate hostesses for some time. But since a good many of the guests who had also been at the concert were in the same condition, there was a sympathetic at-

139

mosphere. Marian herself was in high spirits and hungry, which is always a good beginning for a party, and before it ended, incredibly enough, we were all discussing the same piquant problem which had evoked the lady's confidence about the Turk. What in the opposite sex attracted one?

I remembered it a few nights later at another party.

Chapter Nine

For the sake of our *amour propre* I should like to insinu-
ate the information that by this time our social status
had improved still more. But I do not know how to convey this more subtly than to say that we were beginning
to know more people and to be invited to parties. It was
at Arthur Hornblow's that the matter of attraction came
up again. Dinner had been very entertaining; the food
delicious; Reginald Gardiner, whose imitations, in the
theatre, of wallpaper, armchairs, angry locomotives and
the like are for me, among the immortal pictures of the
world—told, with illustrations, good stories; and Rafaelson,
whom I identified (after he told me) as the playwright
of Gertrude Lawrence's *Skylark*, was interesting. The
women left the men, and went into the drawing room.
One of us was an attractive dark, black-haired, enormous-
eyed girl called Bubbles. She was petulant about her nick-
name, preferring, she said, to be called by her actual
name. But her mother had said it was too big for such a
little baby; so she was called Bubbles. I felt I would not
have been as interested in the mother, had her name not

been Schinasi. But I wondered if she were also an American who had been attracted by the hands of a Turk, or what nationality was she. What nationality was Schinasi? I asked one of the other women.

"I don't know," she said. "Tobacco importers, I think."

Once more I seemed to be the only one interested in nationalities. I explained to myself that it was because I liked people and was curious about them. If I sat next to a Swede at dinner, I wanted to find out how things were in Sweden. At a party a few nights before, one of the women turned out to have gone to Smith, and her husband was a classmate of the host's at Amherst. So we had ended up by singing Smith and Amherst and Bryn Mawr songs, with the Smith girl playing the piano and a man from the cast of *This Is the Army* joining in the choruses. Cornelia and I had also rendered, to our mutual pleasure, a few of the selections, alto and soprano, with which we had held spellbound the inmates of the Paris pension in 1923—*You Can't Git Lovin' Where There Ain't Any Love* and *Come Down the Road to Honeymoon Town.* None of us had participated in just that kind of a musical evening for years, and if I hadn't found out about the guest who had gone to Smith, we wouldn't have had it.

If I hadn't asked about one of the other guests, too, I should never have known that he was a one-time Catholic priest in high office in the church at Rome, who had suddenly become doubtful about a theologic point, left the priesthood and the church, married, had five or six children, and was now acting character parts in the movies—mostly clerical. He also wrote learned articles, since he was a distinguished scholar. At the moment I was told this, the scholar was kissing the under side of Cornelia's arm between the wrist and elbow, and I thought his history interesting.

The men joined us, and some time after that another couple arrived at the house. They had been, I gathered, at a concert together and so could not come to dinner. I did not hear the name of either of them. The man came over and sat beside me on the couch. He was small, with a big head, and beautiful hands, I noticed. But beyond that I was not particularly aware of any characteristic, until suddenly, like a bell, the memory of our ridiculous, adolescent discussions at the other parties rang in my mind. This man beside me, whoever he was, had that outgoing spark which makes for congeniality. He was pleasant looking, cultivated, humorous; he told things well; and he listened courteously and with interest—a form of manners I found rare in Hollywood. Still it was not those gifts which made me like him at once; it was rather a quality of humility, as if he felt it were terribly nice to find himself there and he must do whatever he could to make his coming in late unobtrusive, and yet agreeable to everyone. I wanted to say to him, "Look, I am strange here, too, and I like the way you approach all these Hollywood people."

I was just getting around to it, when Cornelia leaned over from her chair on the opposite side of the fireplace and whispered, "What will you take to change places with me?" I shook my head. "Please," she insisted, "I'm so dying to talk about a play." I suppose I looked blank, because she added in the tone of one whose endurance is shredded to a single frail strand, "That is Behrman, S. N. Behrman. He wrote *The Pirate*, and *No Time For Comedy*, and *Biography*, and——"

I knew what Behrman had written, but I did not know, of course, that this was he. I got up immediately and changed places with her, prompted by no sense of generosity, but by an annoyance at them both. I had wanted to be the one to tell Cornelia, and everyone else when I got home to Philadelphia, that I had discovered a man, just happened to run in to him, sat next to him at a party in fact, who had more charm than all the famous people in Hollywood put together.

In spite, however, of his being famous and my disappointment over it, he did ask us both to lunch with him the next day in Mr. Hornblow's office at Metro-Goldwyn-Mayer. Mr. Hornblow was surprised but brave—a man of unshakable poise. He was in the midst of telling a story when he heard the invitation, and without the sacrifice of so much as a comma, managed to convey by pantomime his pleasure at entertaining us again within the next twenty-four hours.

Why Mr. Hornblow's story led Reginald Gardiner to describe the movie short of Bernard Shaw I do not remember, but it did. What I do remember is his way of telling it. Had we seen it, he asked. Only Mr. Behrman had, and that made Mr. Gardiner very happy because he wanted to tell us about it. The picture began, he said, with nobody in sight at all. There were only a gravel path and some shrubbery, but presently from behind the shrubbery—and there the narrative ceased. Mr. Gardiner made a sound impossible to reproduce and yet familiar. Mr. Behrman interpreted it in an incredulous whisper. "That's the sound of footsteps on a gravel path." That is what it was, indeed, and Mr. Gardiner was not really concerned with the rest of the story. What had fascinated him had been the sound of footsteps on gravel. I suppose no one but a man who interprets the sound of wallpaper, armchairs, and menacing locomotives would have been sensitive to that aspect, but it was the medium in which he told it.

The unobtrusive little woman who had come in with Mr. Behrman, and heretofore taken no part in the conversation, observed that she had stayed with the Shaws when she had gone to London at the age of seventeen to get a feature story about him. She turned out to be Sonia Levien, one of the early and brilliant editors of the

145

Metropolitan Magazine, and her reminiscences of Shaw were engaging. I was perfectly happy for her to turn out to be famous, but I was still soured when I left the party, that the lovely man I had discovered should be somewhat known to other people.

Cornelia and I drove out to the Metro-Goldwyn-Mayer studios the next day for our luncheon engagement. We had by this time rented a drive-it-yourself car. Taxis were very difficult to get, and walking had proven unsatisfactory. Only a few days before we had tried it again from the studio to the hotel aware, by now, of the distance and the length of time it would take, so that I was braced. Chest up, I was testing out a sort of springy step on the balls of my feet which, I told Cornelia, I had read was the method advocated for covering long distances.

But, in the midst of my illustrated lecture, I had caught sight suddenly of calla lilies growing wild among the weeds in the yard of a dilapidated and deserted bungalow, their blooms, like wax bells, heavy on the stalks, high above the matted grass. I had never picked calla lilies, and I gathered an arm load of them, telling Cornelia that I should never forget doing this, and that there was certainly something symbolic about the purity of those flawless, ivory blossoms reaching so high above the squalor below. She said it sounded to her like bad Scott Fitzgerald, or Thomas Burke, maybe, and somebody else said, "Well!" That was the owner of the bungalow and

146

I HAD NEVER PICKED CALLA LILIES, AND I GATHERED AN
ARM LOAD OF THEM, TELLING CORNELIA THAT I SHOULD
NEVER FORGET DOING THIS.

the property, which was anything but abandoned, and he was standing on his own porch watching me. I presented him with my arm load of his lilies and explained to him how much it had meant to me to pick them. Cornelia, at the first and only word from him, had walked quickly on toward the hotel. I preferred, I had told her, when I had finally caught up, not to walk past that place again, and inasmuch as it was the only route back from Paramount without going a considerable distance out of our way, it brought the whole matter of transportation to a peak, and we rented a car.

But I drove it. Cornelia's technique is too reminiscent of her approach to the typewriter—a peck on the accelerator, and then an anxious survey ahead to see what it has accomplished. She insists, however, though I consider it irrelevant, that I include my own confusion about the car.

We rented one, but Phyllis Povah told us about a cheaper place, so we rented one from there. Then I telephoned the owner of the first car to come to the hotel and get it. But I mistook the two cars—after all, we had taken them both within forty-eight hours—and I drove the first car to the studio, instead of leaving it to be called for. At the end of the day, when the studio garage man brought it out, I still thought it was, of course, the first car, only, I noticed, it had no rumble seat. I told the garage man the seat must have been taken. He was very noisy about what the hell would he or anyone want with

a rumble seat, and were we trying to give him a run-
around. It was an uncomfortable minute or two.

And when we got home, the hotel garage man said that
the owner of the first car had come for it, and it was not
there. Stolen, of course, I thought, and telephoned the
police at once. The garage man was the one who discovered that I was driving the first car—the second did have
a rumble seat, just as I remembered. By that time the
police and the owner were there, and it took a little time
to straighten out the situation. Nevertheless, when I am
in the driving seat of a car, no matter *whose* car it is, I
am more competent than Cornelia.

I love the trick photography in a movie which reduces
an individual to the size of a mouse and makes his environment "super-terrific." I experienced a little of it at
Metro-Goldwyn-Mayer, and I do not care for it in real
life. We got out of our car, two women among other
women and men, but by the time we had crossed the
parking area the size of a stadium, persisted to the main
entrance, after two or three sallies into wrong buildings,
I felt the approximate stature of the sorcerer's apprentice
in *Fantasia*. I told the receptionist in some anxiety that
we were there to see Mr. Hornblow and Mr. Behrman.

And they were there to see us, too, bless them—not
loose among the corridors but safe in their offices where
trained guides could lead parties to them. Along the un-
charted corridors I saw the names of writers I thought

149

were dead. I don't suppose they are, but it is conceivable to me that they are lost.

Mr. Hornblow's offices included a library, dining room, and kitchen. Beyond this suite was another room which might have been an office, inasmuch as Mr. Behrman told us he was using that to work in. The library looked out across the entrance and the parking tract. Mr. Hornblow said he had been watching our approach from that window. He must have used a spy-glass. Mr. Hornblow himself is very handsome and has great style. He makes me feel that either there are really such people as those we have seen for years in drawing room plays, or else that he himself is in one—of charming manners— playing very deftly, and with ease.

Mr. Behrman came hurrying in from his work room. He told us that Arthur had been somewhat dismayed to find that the luncheon was being given in his office. He had been, Mr. Behrman added quickly, most cooperative about entertaining us, but had never before had a meal served in his offices. Mr. Behrman felt that was a great pity. A dining room, after all, *was* there, a very handsome room, and it seemed wasteful to use it only to walk through. Mr. Hornblow assured us that he was delighted to use it, only, as a housekeeper, he was a little dubious about its appointments. But perhaps we would think of it as a picnic. A Filipino boy served us, or was supposed to, but since he actually arrived only with the dessert and without any forks for it, we were not dependent upon him. The pie for dessert had been Mr. Behrman's idea. It made a party, he said, more substantial. You remembered it longer. The pie tasted like a sort of apple-butterscotch-mince, and since I generally lunch on cold meat, salad, and a slice of Melba toast, I remembered it for a long time. I remember it even now vividly.

I had heard that Mr. Behrman was working on a picture version of *Quo Vadis*. It seemed to me an incongruous selection for a master of polished comedy, and I asked how it was coming along. He was fascinated, he said, by the early Christians. He had never seen nor heard of people so preoccupied with dying and getting such pleasure out of it. It seemed to be all they lived for. His people, he added thoughtfully, had been actively concerned with dying over a very long time, but he couldn't say that he thought they had ever relished it. I remembered this—and the weary humor of his voice and his eyes when he said it—more acutely than anything else of the day—except, perhaps, the pie.

I talked again about his people a few nights later at a party which an old friend and her husband gave. When I first knew her years ago, she was unmarried. She had then a glorious sense of clowning, a lightning quick sympathy, and an equally lightning quick descent into a brooding melancholy, which never permitted the restfulness of a single dull moment in her company. She was more beautiful this time than when I had known her before, and very much happier. She told me this herself the moment I arrived at the party. "I am," she announced, "much happier than when you knew me. That was because I was trying to get my husband, and I didn't know whether I was going to be able to or not. But I did get him, and I've never regretted it, but then I never thought I would."

The talk about her people did not come up until later in the evening. At dinner I sat next to Michael Arlen. He turned out to be a nice, dependable, family man. There was a reminiscent tickle with the feather of *The Green Hat* when he said that no woman was really attractive to a man when she was thin, wore a hat, or her hair down; but for the rest, he was domestic. He would not have mentioned his books, I am sure, if I had not. I think he was pleased to talk about Lily Christine, but, he said, there was no place in this world for his heroines, or his books. They were gone, with another world.

We talked, too, a little about his being an Armenian. He had invented the name Arlen, he said, and had worked over it a long time. His own name was unpronounceable, and he made up his mind to have one that would be easy to remember and yet not be commonplace. Armen was his first choice, a derivative of Armenian, but the sound did not please him. Then he hit upon Arlen. Before he actually adopted it, however, he looked in the telephone directory of every large city in the world, and there was not a single Arlen listed.

But in Hollywood one day, when he had come out after the success of *The Green Hat,* an actor had approached him and asked if he might take the name of Arlen. Would Mr. Arlen object? It had a pleasant sound, was easy to remember, very good for advertising—in fact, a perfect movie name. Mr. Arlen had had very much the same ideas in mind when he had worked it out for himself, and spent considerable time on it, but he did not see how he could refuse to share his product; and so he did, with Richard Arlen.

Today, he said, there are some hundred and fifty Arlens in the London telephone directory, a good many in the New York, and a considerable number listed in cities all over the country—and not, he interpolated hastily, due to any personal prowess of his own nor Mr. Richard Arlen's —but because at least that many other people had been nameless or dissatisfied, and liked the syllables of Arlen. It was a very curious thing, he said, to watch the growth of a family in which there were no relatives.

He was, I told him, the first person I had met in Hollywood who had mentioned his birthplace. As far as that went, I said, I had not heard anyone mention it about anyone else, and just then the hostess got up from the table and herded the women out of the dining room.

When the rest of them were talking among themselves,

she moved with me to another part of the room, and the very thing she wanted to talk about was what I had just told Mr. Arlen, that I hadn't heard mentioned—nationality or race. She was concerned, she said, for her children. I reminded her of the story she had once told me that her Irish nurse, angry at the family, had whisked the baby around the corner to the Catholic church and had her baptized, returning home then in a gentle and forgiving mood with the little Catholic baby. My friend's mother had not, of course, known of the excursion until she was waited upon by a pair of sisters come to check on the religious training of their little parishioner.

The same thing had happened to her husband, my friend said; only he had not discovered it until they had been about to be married. It had been quite unhandy. But Irish nurses, whenever they got mad at their employers, were always doing that to little Jew babies. She went back to the matter of her own children. You couldn't laugh now, she challenged, about a little Jewish kid in the Catholic church. You couldn't laugh much about it anywhere. What did I think was the solution?

I didn't know, I told her, but I did think there was something different about Hollywood—something I couldn't put my finger on—but it was important.

The men joined us and some additional guests arrived. They had been asked to come in after dinner. One of them, a woman, small and blond, had on tight fitting black cloth trousers like a Spanish dancer's (male), a tighter fitting black sweater, the kind worn by a college crew (male), a superb string of pearls, and a half dozen or so magnificent diamond bracelets.

The hostess moved off to settle the new arrivals, and the man who sat down beside me started at once to tell a story about an author across the room from us. He had, my minstrel began—and there seemed to be no effort toward privacy about it—taken on some fixed and strenuous alcoholic habits which brought him to a doctor's office abysmally below par. The doctor advised a cure immediately in a sanitarium for that purpose, and the patient agreed on condition that it be done at once, while he was still feeling ill enough to be acquiescent. The doctor accordingly took him to the sanitarium, where he was promptly incarcerated, but allowed to make one telephone call to his wife to inform her of his change of address. She was, understandably, bemused, but, trying to assume a mastery of the situation, asked what he would need in such a place that she could bring him.

And the unhappy patient had replied, "I can't think what it would be, unless maybe my three-cornered hat, my sword, my portrait of Josephine, and a pound of bird seed."

Hollywood conversation is almost entirely anecdotal.

Chapter Ten

I thought again about my conversation with my friend, however, lying awake in bed in my hotel the next morning waiting to telephone. Every Sunday morning I called the twins at home. Half-past seven Philadelphia time I had found was an hour in which calls would go through most easily. The twins, Sunday or not, were always up at that time. And so I talked to them at half-past four every Sunday, Hollywood time. As a matter of fact, I invariably wakened at four. And that half hour while I waited to pick up the telephone was my favorite time in the week —better, almost than the call itself. Then I would be anxious about asking all the things I had made a note of to ask, apprehensive that I would not hear all that each one wanted to tell me, or that we would be cut off, frantic over the inevitable silences in which none of us could think of anything to say. So the call itself was always a little disappointing. Like the first few hours of a friend's visit to which you have been looking forward for weeks. After the fanfare of greeting, and then the baggage checking, you don't know where to start or what to talk about, and wonder why you ever asked her. Only the visit gets better after those first few hours, while the telephone conversation is all over and you can't improve on it.

But lying in bed, waiting for it, I could watch the black outline of the eucalyptus trees outside my window, see the sky run through with the first broken strand of light like a basting thread, hear the birds begin to be aware of it, and occasionally the hush of a car going by on the wet streets below. I do not know whether it rains every Saturday night or whether there is a heavy dew, but the cars always sounded as if the streets were wet.

The twins, I knew, would be tip-toeing about their rooms on the third floor, conscientiously trying not to disturb other people. At home it always sounded to me, in the room below, as if they tip-toed on the backs of their heels. B would be apprehensive, too, about the phone call they were expecting because it would involve so many complications. Should they risk going out to feed their rabbits and ducks first? Then maybe they wouldn't hear the telephone. But, on the other hand, if they waited for the telephone, the call might be delayed, and then they would be late getting the animals fed. A would be completely indifferent to all of this, and this would further B's sense of slight exasperation. But B would not realize that A was indifferent because she was churned up inside. It had taken *me* a long time to understand that, when A's emotions were threatened, she carried them to a safe hiding place, and then put on an act like a mother

157

partridge trailing a broken wing to lead you away. That was why, of course, when A was very little she had been so obstreperous on the way to the doctor's where she knew she was to be given an injection or something that might hurt. Her high spirits and mischievousness would lead you away from the place where she was scared. But B's insides were not churned into confusion that way. She is as generous with them as she is with everything else, bringing you her anger, her pleasure, her grief, without even waiting to wrap them. There is nothing in the world she loves better than giving presents. She had sent me two or three that week, wrapped in pieces of kleenex, and I made a note in the dark that I must be sure to remember to thank her for them.

There were more basting threads of light in the sky now. In a few minutes I could put the call through. It was such anguish to hear their voices—blithe spirits so far away I could not touch them, nor see how dirty their nails were so that they would have to go back upstairs and scrub their hands again, nor smell their sweatiness when they came in from a game of tether ball, and make them stay out of a draft until they cooled off. But it wasn't such anguish as my friend's, who *could* hold and see and smell her children, and be afraid about them—afraid of what was going to happen to them because they were Jews, proud, beautiful, intelligent, sensitive Jews. And yet who in Hollywood cared? No one I had met. Like a box on the ears, the realization hit me of what it was that I had tried to tell her, the difference I felt between Hollywood and the East—a difference that was so great as to make me aware of it constantly and naggingly, and not until this instant able to identify it. It was this—the INdifference of Hollywood, the indifference to any race or nationality or color.

It is much easier to recognize something that *is* there than to identify something that is not. A friend of mine was in Stockholm for a week before she could put her finger on the reason why it was not like any other city she had ever seen. The reason was the *absence* of the poor. There weren't any. When you have grown up under the acceptance of "the poor are always with us," the negative of that is a shock.

In Hollywood—and *I* had been so long in recognizing it —the Armenians, the Turks, the Negroes, French, Egyptians, Jews, Czechoslovakians—whatever—were not with us either. Neither with us, nor, for that matter, against us. They simply did not exist as such. And so there was no issue about them, because you could not make an issue of something you did not even notice. We did notice them in the East—all nationalities, and races and colors—and the reason we did was because birthplace and habitat made up the common denominator of our, at least, social conversation.

A few days before, I had gone to a party given by some

people not associated with pictures. "Private people" Charlie Brackett says they are called by the motion picture set. Friends of mine in Philadelphia had written to them, and they had responded handsomely with a tea. Every single person, man or woman, there had told me either some or all of these things: his or her city and country of birth, where educated, and where they went for the summer. Those statistics were, of course, what we had in common.

But that was not what the motion picture people had in common, and I had been such a dolt to have fumbled about it for as long as this. Everyone in the movie colony of Hollywood had come with a job to do. And who cared *where* they had come from? The job was their common ground. Their beginning had no value; their ability, their specialty—those were identification tags which really priced them.

I suddenly remembered one night two or three winters ago when I had met Paul Robeson at Bryn Mawr College after a concert he had given there. A few people had been asked to stay on, and we sat in the Deanery, talking. Some time in that conversation he had asked me if *I* could suggest anywhere other than Russia where his child could be brought up unaware of differences of creed or race or color. I had no other suggestion then, but I wouldn't be afraid now to suggest Hollywood. Hollywood —that cheap, crass, vulgar place, as you read about it,

160

where Paul Robeson had been only the week before to give a talk on the future of the Negro and had asked Sheridan Gibney where he might speak. And Sheridan and Mildred, his gentle, lovely wife—had offered their house and given a party. And for four or five days before, Sheridan's secretary, Rose, had had to get someone else to take our dictation in order to be free to answer the incessant telephone calls of people clamoring to come to Sheridan's house.

I had, myself, after all, given a party for Marian Anderson, to which people had been eager to come. And not until this second had I realized that it never crossed my mind to question the possibility of having the party at my hotel, much less allow for a possible color prejudice among my guests. I should have, I knew to my shame, been aware of it in the East. But in this community of Hollywood, at least that part which concerns itself with motion pictures, Marian Anderson, being one of the greatest artists in the world, was, therefore, someone, of course, whom it was a privilege to meet.

I had heard about another artist in Hollywood. Everyone who talked about her—and almost everyone did— was surprised that I did not know her. When I'd finally met her I found she was a Negress. Not one person had mentioned it.

I had asked a man where so-an-so, whose English was almost too uncertain to understand, came from. The man had been surprised. "Don't you know about him? He did some beautiful work in New York."

Obviously, I'd not met everyone in motion picture Hollywood, but this was the impression I'd gotten from those I *had* met—a very strong impression. The conversation, I may have thought, was anecdotal, but it was not ancestral.

Yes, I should say, Paul Robeson could bring his wife and child along and settle here. So could anyone from anywhere so long as he had just one thing—a talent, or an appreciation of talent. And their children would grow up to be more American than in any other community I had happened to see in this country, an American being, of course, the product of a residence, not a birthplace. And a citizen of a motion-picture Hollywood is far too busy and occupied with other things to think of asking what the newest resident was before he became one of them. That is what makes a Hollywood citizen so different.

I picked up the telephone and heard the call go through across the country. I heard Chicago answer, and then Philadelphia, and then Ardmore 3467, and B's voice saying anxiously "Is that you, Mommy? The bands are on my teeth and they're very painful." The voice had the note of a lark, because nothing is more pleasing to B than to participate in the mode, and to fulfill every detail of the conventional pattern. To have bands on her teeth was a real fulfillment. A, she went on, not so exhilarated, was out in the garden, although B had told her not to go away from the telephone. I could have told B that I was quite sure A had stayed by the telephone until she had actually heard it ring, and that had been a little too much for her, so she had darted into the garden to hide her emotion and her excitement somewhere. Sure enough, B announced, "Well, here she comes. Hurry up, A, Mommy's on the telephone."

"Hello, Mommy," A said, and her voice was a little bit shaky. "The Chinese are very interesting people, don't you think they are? I have a joke for you, too."

I went to sleep again after I had finished talking to them, and it was late when I woke up, barely time to get dressed for lunch at the Nigel Bruces'. And that, together with the party that night at Mr. Charles Coburn's, turned out to be two functions of such characteristically national feeling that each household could have waved its respective flag out the window and not been any more clearly stamped.

The party at the Bruces' was "brunch" at half-past twelve. Nigel stood on the doorstep to welcome us with open arms. He is stocky, ruddy, beetle-browed (whatever in the world that is) and blue-eyed. I never heard his voice when it was not husky and a little hoarse, and yet I have always the impression that he has been *roaring* commands, jokes, complaints, tender sentiments until just the minute I happen to hear him, when he must have lost his voice temporarily from strain. He was so completely the English squire welcoming us that it seemed a pity not to have behind him a train of boys carrying yule logs and boars' heads, and singing waits. He stumped ahead, showing us the way into the big drawing room, calling out, like the clerk of the courtroom, that we were coming. Since we had been in view from the moment we stepped out of the car, the announcement may have been superfluous, but it definitely added to the general trend of hospitality and welcome. Nigel was limping quite badly, and carried a cane. We did not learn for some time the reason for this, because it took patience and ingenuity to unravel the theme from his sonorous and angry variations. Clipped of impatience and exasperation, however, it was that he had been on a bond selling tour for the Government which had laid him up for three weeks in bed with a recurrence of an old leg wound from the last war. This was his first time downstairs, allowed him on condition that he keep very quiet. The only time during the day that I saw him even sit down for a period of three minutes or more, was when he was eating lunch.

Bunny, Nigel's wife, small, dark, pretty, and one of the most patient women I have ever seen, reminded me hauntingly of Tante—Mrs. Skinner. Curiously enough, I was about to say that Bunny reminded me of several people out of Barrie's plays, and I remember that Winthrop Ames said to Tante, "Maude, you weren't born;

Barrie wrote you." Tante was a more intellectual person than I think perhaps Bunny is, but then, Mr. Skinner was a quieter man, which must have given her more time. But Bunny has a very feminine charm, and also a charm of *non sequitur* conversation, very like Tante's.

We met the two daughters immediately, both of them tearing beauties. They were very heavily made up, just as the Charlie Bracketts' daughter (who has the most beautiful eyes I ever looked at) had been each time I saw her. I don't suppose any of these girls was over twenty, and yet they had on at lunch, or at any time of the day for that matter, a make-up which would have withstood the most searching light of the studio. In Hollywood it was not particularly noticeable, not because that type of make-up was common to everyone out there—I never saw it, outside of the studios, on any but young girls for whom it was evidently the current mode—but because in Hollywood, like practically everything else, it was not noticed. When you have seen men walking down the main boulevard, two of them, in white robes, high turbans, sandals on their bare feet, and beards across their chests, and the head of not a single passer-by so much as swerve, you begin to have a feeling, slightly uneasy, that you could go out of your mind trying to attract attention in Hollywood, and even that would not arouse their notice. Just another aspect, perhaps, of the color-nationality-race indifference of the place. I wondered, too, if spending the greater part of your life among people made up to look like another personality or type would not make you profoundly indifferent both to make-up and the type itself when you met them outside.

The girls went with Bunny into the kitchen for the last rounding up of brunch. They were also, like everyone else in Hollywood, without a cook. We were left with Nigel to meet the other guests, all of them men and all of them nameless for that day, though Nigel did wave his hand at them and at us in a sort of get-together implication, and rumbled something which might have been, "I expect you know all these people, what?" But he was impatient. He wanted to settle down and did, to an inch-by-inch description of the arrival of four puppies the night before from their dachshund bitch. As the cord of the last one was severed, Bunny called us to the dining room.

I could keep just as accurate a record of the remainder of that day without putting down another word about it. All I need do is paste in the pages from *Our Hearts Were Young and Gay* which described our Sunday at the H. G. Wells' in England. The only difference was that Nigel, who is divinely funny both intentionally and unintentionally, did not make very bad puns like Mr. Wells, and he did not shout us into intellectual gymnastics. He and darling Bunny, however, did whirl us into a game as we rose from the table, and it was a special game and we were especially bulging with food. It was the Bruce game—

just as we had played the Wells game. The basis was ping pong but the rules were the Bruces'. Furthermore there was a chart drawn up of just how the tournament was to be run, which would have done credit to any major tennis club. And when the finals were played, Nigel and one of the daughters were the survivors. You might have thought that since the members of the family were in the habit of playing with one another every day throughout the year, the match lacked novelty and might even have petered out. Not at all. They played as if they had never faced each other before; and furthermore Bunny and the other daughter pulled their chairs up to the side lines and watched with an intensity which would have done them proud at Wimbledon. And they sat in complete silence, no talking between them except for an occasional cry of "Well played—oh, very well played." The rest of us were in a far part of the garden prostrated with discomfort after our lesser matches. But the Bruces paid no attention to us whatsoever until the final point of the tournament was played. Then Nigel, marching over proudly and with great excitement, announced himself the winner. No one else, it turned out, ever had won at a Bruce tournament, but the cries of pleasure and surprise of his family were hearty and genuine.

Almost immediately after this we had tea. Tea was a little congested because Bunny rushed us all into a small library. She saw, she said, a new cook coming up the path to be interviewed, who looked, too, a terrible swell. Bunny did not, she announced, wish her to be put off by us. She also wished to convey that the Bruces' was a small, home-loving family, finding entertainment among themselves. Since several people had dropped in during the ping pong tournament, the original party had now increased to some twenty-odd. We were distributed in the library in a way which reminded me of the old game of "Sardines." But we kept very quiet while Bunny entertained in the drawing room.

We were locked in so long, however (the cook decided in the end that the place wouldn't quite suit, and drove away in her car), that Cornelia and I had barely time to get home and dress for Mr. Coburn's dinner. And just as we were leaving, a message came through that Alden, who was expected the next day, had got an earlier plane and was at that moment coming into the airport. Cornelia rushed off to meet him and I went on alone.

All of this had made me late, and when I came into his apartment, the other guests had arrived. But my shyness lasted only a minute. Out of the silence, as the guests all looked up to see the new arrival, one of them spoke and I recognized, even in my confusion, that it was Spring Byington.

"Well," she said, "you don't look a bit the way you did in the book."

That brought Mr. Coburn from the dining room, where

168

SHE SAW, SHE SAID, A NEW COOK COMING UP THE PATH
TO BE INTERVIEWED, WHO LOOKED, TOO, A TERRIBLE
SWELL. BUNNY DID NOT, SHE ANNOUNCED, WISH HER TO
BE PUT OFF BY US.

he had been putting the finishing touches on the table. From the moment he took my hand and led me from each guest to the next, introducing us carefully (and a greater contrast to the meeting of guests at the Bruces could scarcely be imagined), it was a Southern party, with the warmth and the geniality and the story-telling that could only have been born and raised there. And when more friends came in after dinner, they were the *neighbors*, not geographically perhaps, but in the sense that in the South when you have a visitor from out of town, your friends come around. Some of these neighbors were Beulah Bondi, Zasu Pitts, James Rennie, Pedro de Cordoba and a great many other familiar names—but a great many more I never did identify. They had just run in to make the visitors feel at home and to do honor to their neighbor, Charlie, who was having an evening party.

When we slipped away, because we had to be at work early in the morning, they were still coming. It had been a long day for me, starting at four in the morning when I lay in the dark, thinking about Hollywood American citizens. And the end was the sight of Mr. Coburn, standing at the head of the stairs to welcome, with the hospitality born in the South, his Hollywood neighbors. But only God knew where all of them had been born.

Chapter Eleven

A few of my friends in the East had urged me not to go to Hollywood because of the war. It's much more dangerous there, they said, than the Atlantic seaboard. Due to my geographic ineptitude, one ocean is much like another to me, and if I were looking for a place in which to feel safest, I would take a twin under each arm and make for the corn fields of Indiana.

I did expect Hollywood to be tense about the war, however, partly because it was actually vulnerable, perhaps, and partly because it would be, temperamentally, Hollywood, of course. But this was the first of the Hollywood indifferences which I encountered. Hollywood was completely indifferent to any *actuality* of war close to home. It was exclusively preoccupied with the *theatre* of war all over the world. It was true that in every building there were elaborate instructions for procedure in an air raid, and an air raid warden did ask me, in the event of a raid, to meet him on the roof, but that rendezvous never came off. What was much more highly featured than where to go in the event of a bomb, was where to go to buy a bond. Every billboard was papered with dramatic posters; every

171

pay check was accompanied by an urgent reminder amounting almost to a command. The campaign was extremely well organized, and of course superbly dramatized. All productions, too, were aimed at the war theatre. If *Lady in the Dark* and *Let's Face It* were not actually war pictures, they were certainly aimed at the boys. All the rest of them which I saw in production—*Five Graves to Cairo, So Proudly We Hail, China*—were war. A play-war, I thought, just what you would expect of the Hollywood you read about, a whooped-up, sensational, emotional, over-dramatized play war, with no awareness whatsoever of the real thing—just actors in phony uniforms and fake, bloody bandages, going through a make-believe bombardment. And they would not get any nearer to its reality at home at the end of the day. Exhausted by the strain of it all, too tired to read the papers, much too tired to go out, they would be able only to fall into bed and cut off the telephone. The trouble about my ideas of this sort is that I have to take back so many of them.

There are not many people outside of the actual fighting forces *more* conscious of the reality of the war than the motion picture actors. They are aware of it when, after a long day's work at the studio, they bump some hundred and fifty miles in a big truck to give a performance at an army camp, and back again in the early hours before dawn to be on the lot for work by six o'clock. They know it at the Hollywood Canteen where, after a long day at the studio, they serve soft drinks, put on an act, and sing, until the place closes. They must be conscious of it when they barnstorm across the country on a bond selling tour, speaking wherever and whenever a crowd is collected, or when they turn up at every fighting front to toss off an entertainment, until, as has happened to any number of them, they drop in their tracks and are carted off to the nearest hospital. When they recover sufficiently, they go on again. These, of course, are the ones not in active service, although a less inactive way of serving would be hard to imagine. The ones in the literal and actual fighting service are occasionally brought back, fighting like mules, to do a war picture, made at the order of the Government.

Frieda Inescort, who is an old friend of ours, asked Cornelia to do a monologue or two at the Canteen, and Cornelia, of course, said she would be delighted. The performance was set for the following Saturday night. On Monday or Tuesday of that week Miss Bette Davis' secretary telephoned. Miss Davis wished to know, she said, if Miss Skinner would go to the Canteen on Saturday as her guest. Miss Skinner, I told her (I had happened to answer the telephone), was going on Saturday evening—Miss Frieda Inescort had asked her. But, said the persistent secretary, Miss Davis would be disappointed if Miss Skinner were not *her* guest. Did Miss Skinner know that Miss Davis was asking her? No, I told her, Miss Skinner undoubtedly did not know (Miss Skinner at the moment being in the bathtub several rooms away, and not endowed either with supernatural hearing nor with a faculty for telepathy). But even under such handicaps Miss Skinner would still be delighted, I assured the secretary, to perform at the Canteen, but happened to be going with Miss Inescort. In bewilderment and sorrow, reiterating that Miss Davis would be very disappointed, the secretary rang off.

A few days later at a party at Lady Mendl's, one of the guests called across the room that she wanted to talk to me. I had been spellbound by the height of her blue-black lacquered pompadour. She understood, she said, that Cornelia and I were coming to the Canteen on Saturday night, and that Cornelia was going to do a monologue or two. She hoped I would come, too, and sit in the space provided for the very few spectators admitted. I said, of course, that I should be delighted, and I learned later that she, little, delicate, looking as if she lived like mushrooms and breast of guinea hen—"sous clôche"—was not only indefatigable at the Canteen itself, but could raise money with the power of a dredge.

Lady Mendl hopped over to us a few minutes later. She is like a magpie—sharp, friendly, handsome, with an insatiable curiosity. Was it true, she asked, that Cornelia was going to do a monologue at the Canteen on Saturday night? She wanted to be sure to be there if it were. When she had hopped away again, satisfied, someone said that it was a wonderful and terrifying sight to see her at work in the Canteen. She was quicker, she worked harder, she was gayer than almost anyone there of any age. And it was no use worrying about whether she would drop dead or not, because she wouldn't.

Then I saw Mrs. Sam Goldwyn across the room and went to speak to her. Back in the days just after Cornelia and I returned from Paris, Mrs. Sam Goldwyn, who was Frances Howard then, used to pose for Eugene Hutchinson, the photographer, in Chicago. I got a job on *Fashions of the Hour,* the magazine Marshall Field published, and we used to photograph Frances. She saw me at almost the same moment, and before we had actually reached each other, we were talking about the old days, when Frances started a whole new type of photography. And she *had* launched a thousand plates, or more, because one morning in Eugene Hutchinson's studio she stuck her head out of the dressing room to hear what he was saying and she happened to have a towel tight around her head to protect her hair when she took off her dress. Mr. Hutchinson stopped what *he* was saying, and bawled to her to come on out quick, the way she was. He photographed her head with a towel around it against a white background. In the finished picture he faded out the towel completely so that there was nothing but the beautifully chiseled face, fading out into whiteness. He put it

175

in his window and it created a minor riot among photographic circles. Up to that moment backgrounds had been so filled with potted palms, lattice work with vines up and down, couches, chairs, fireplaces, screens, mirrors, that it was hard to find the figures at all. But Frances' face stripped photography.

We gathered quite a little group around us, talking of those days, when Eva Le Gallienne, posing for the magazine, found nothing in the store which she felt suitable for her to wear, but, persuaded that a page in the store magazine must bear some relationship to the store merchandise, consented magnanimously to be cooperative, and selected a prie-dieu from the antique department, on which she knelt. We did not anticipate doing a very large mail order business in prie-dieux, and we were not disappointed. But there was Edna Best, I reminded Frances, on the other hand, who was willing and delighted to wear anything we asked her, but who revealed, when she pulled her own blue serge dress off, that she was wearing nothing whatever underneath it, and the dress buyer was so shaken at the sight that she about-faced and assisted Miss Best to put on the Marshall Field apparel by a peculiar touch system with her hands behind her back.

Cornelia broke in to say that she was sorry to bring us out of the past, but that, in this dull present, we *were* going to the Academy dinner, and had better go home to dress. *That* started something. What were we going to wear? A rhetorical question, if I ever heard one. They did not want our answer. They wanted to complain. Some trouble-maker had suggested that in a war year elaborate evening dress might make a bad impression, and since all over the country that night the people of America would be glued to their radios to hear a stitch-by-stitch description of every star, the matter of clothes must be thought of as the establishment of a national policy. A late arrival came down the room to our group, calling out her news like the messenger in *Medea*. Norma Shearer, she gasped, spent with the exertion of bringing the tidings in time, had worked out the solution for everybody. She was at that moment having the bottom of an evening dress cut off to street length. From the waist up she would satisfy her fans and from the waist down, her patriotism. Nothing short of inspired, the group pronounced it. Didn't we think so, they appealed to Cornelia and me. We were, I explained apologetically, since we really were expected to answer now, going with Mr. and Mrs. Y. Frank Freeman, and she had *asked* us to wear street dresses and hats. The group made little clucking noises of sympathy and scattered—for their scissors, I suppose.

We were the guests of the Freemans, but Charlie Brackett and his wife drove us to the Ambassador. If my children and I could be warm and clothed and fed, and I could see Elizabeth and Charlie at least once a week, preferably oftener, the year round, I should consider that a thoroughly satisfactory way to live. Elizabeth is all curves, warmth, generosity and affection; and her conversation has just about as much warmth and softness as a buzz saw, with an Indiana accent. She was, as a matter of fact, born in Indiana but that has nothing to do with my extravagant affection for her. On the way to the Ambassador she was cutting through the Academy dinner. One of the greatest indignities, she enumerated, would be that monstrosity which would be set down before each of us, that contradiction to anatomy which was somehow born for every banquet—a breast of chicken with a leg sticking out of the middle of it. And sure enough, the entrée of the Academy banquet was a breast of chicken, with the thigh and lower limbs growing up from its center. She was equally dour about the program of the evening. "Speeches!" she said darkly. "Wait until you hear them."

On the way home she admitted that even in her blackest imagination she had not conceived that a Russian could speak to us in phonetically arranged syllables, possibly English, though we had not recognized one of them, for forty minutes. She was pleased, though, by Mr. Mayer's secret and private wish for his family, confided into the microphone over a coast-to-coast hook-up, that its members, or some of them, might one day grow up to be as famous a man as he had been accounted by this assemblage tonight. I was pleased by every aspect of the spectacle except its length, and our entrance. But then, I have not achieved the scope and grandeur of Elizabeth's malevolence toward humanity at large.

Charlie let us out at the canopied entrance and went off to park the car. The prospect ahead was one, I must admit, which did not please. A carpeted passageway stretched far, far ahead, and it was walled on either side by people who had come to look. The wall was retained only by the strength of the line of policemen on the edge of either side of the carpet, holding hands and the crowd back. There was nothing about the presence of the crowd which depressed me; in fact, I was rather exhilarated by it. As we got out of the car a couple moved into the lighted passage ahead of us, and a yell broke out from the bulging audience. "Yea, Charlie Coburn," the fans roared and screamed shrilly. "And Spring Byington! How're ya, Charlie? Give us a look, Spring. Let me see your dress. Good old Charlie." And at the far end of the passage the flashlight bulbs popped as the news photographers backed away from the couple, photographing as they backed. But there was not a sound nor a pop as Elizabeth, Cornelia and I walked the length of the interminable passage. There was not even so much as a whispered murmur of curiosity inquiring *who* we were—just an exasperated, impatient silence until we should get out of the way and let some more favorites come into view.

179

It was like the time when I got into the middle of a circus parade, by mistake, in the family's electric. I had thought it was the end, but the ranks closed in behind me, and I had had to drive three miles before I could get out. The distance now seemed approximately the same.

We waited for Charlie at the bend of the passage, stepping at last off the red carpet. I found myself engaged almost immediately in conversation with three gentlemen beside me. They were, the one nearest told me, from Minnesota, Michigan, and Kansas; not friends, he explained, just happened to be in the town on business and had run into each other leaving the hotel to take a stroll around to see the sights. And, boy, did they ever think they were going to see a sight like this! It was sure something to take back to the folks. I was pretty lucky, too, to have got in on it. Had I ever seen one of these things before? No, I hadn't. And at that moment Ginger Rogers with her new husband came along the carpet, arousing maniacal screams from her enraptured public. As she came abreast she caught sight of me with my three sight-seeing friends. And with a start of recognition, and a little smile of tolerance she waved to me and my friends and went on. "Well, boy," the man from Michigan told us all, "if that ain't friendly! Not stuck up like some of 'em are, but real approachable with her fans. Wait until I tell my family back home. Tell your people, too," he advised me, "when you get home."

180

It was the peak of the evening for Elizabeth. She and Cornelia were swaying with audible delight. I managed to forget it for a little while at the banquet itself. Mrs. Freeman, whose soft Georgia voice could put charm into the reading of a telephone directory, enumerated the stars in the packed and jammed room—within the immediate radius of our table. Rosalind Russell, at a nearby table, looked very beautiful and very pregnant, as indeed she was. Gary Cooper looked shy and embarrassed, and I was told that he was, always.

Preston Sturges sat on my right, very distinguished and handsome, with one lock of white hair—like Whistler's, and the newest fashion among the debutantes—the rest, very black as to hair, very dark as to skin. He had been one of the first people at Paramount to make me feel welcome, with a lovely warmth and ease, and I shall be grateful to him always. But even he and Mrs. Freeman could not entirely counteract the tedium of the speeches. They stretched in what had every indication of being an endless chain, each serving only to introduce the following representative of the good, the true, the beautiful— the Motion Picture Industry. The only relief, of a sort, from this monotonous procession, was the Russian who read for forty minutes what we supposed to be a speech in Russian, until someone who knew told us that it was in English, written out for him, since he did not know the language—phonetically, and, furthermore, prepared by this lingual zealot, only syllabically, without separation into words.

Bob Hope, however, was the gem and redemption of the platform—spontaneously funny. Cornelia sighed that he was really her dream man, and was promptly taken over by Mr. Freeman to meet Mr. Hope as he came from the platform. The fact that Mr. Freeman prefaced the introduction by quoting what Cornelia had just said, reduced them both to a nervous immobility, like rocks of jello. I found a certain morbid comfort in the sight, soothing to my recollection of the boys and me at the entrance to the party.

Driving home that night, however, Elizabeth reiterated that my sickly grin in return to Ginger's jovial nod to my boy friends and me was the memory of the whole party which she would keep the longest, longer than the memory of Teresa Wright's touchingly sincere burst of tears at being given an Oscar, or Greer Garson's speech of acceptance which she was unable to end, or even Hedda Hopper's hat made of nylon tubes, artificial flowers, and bedsprings, which someone declared was a Dali portrait of Hedda's life. No, far and away the best of all were the four jays from the corn belt—my friends and I.

Obviously, with such goings-on I had not thought again of the Canteen engagement since Lady Mendl's six-inch pompadoured guest had invited me. But on Saturday Cornelia reminded me. You cannot distract her New England stern and rockbound coast line of duty, not even with an Academy dinner. We dined first with Frieda and her husband, Ray Redman, at the Brown Derby, where Cornelia pointed out to us Norman Bel Geddes. He turned out, on closer inspection, to be a tourist of the sort who should certainly have been one of my party at the Academy dinner. But it was quite understandable. The Brown Derby clientele is made up almost entirely of sightseers, come to look at the famous, who are seldom there. But you catch the feeling of expectancy in the air and begin seeing them yourself or improvising them, the way in Paris you used to think that every American you saw must be someone you knew.

We slipped into the Canteen by the back way, and were swarmed over by the usual grimy, whining auto-graph hunters. Not I, of course, but Cornelia and Frieda Inescort. The kitchen and passage-way were jammed with men and women carrying trays, washing dishes, and I recognized one or two movie people among them. Edward Knopf looked up from some job and called hello. My Madame la Pompadour came working her way through the crowd to take our party; and while someone else took Cornelia along to the side room where the performers waited their turn, she pushed and coaxed a way for the rest of us through as densely packed a slice of human beings as I think I have ever seen. But there was a little raised platform in the back of the room, with chairs and a table, and we were eventually harbored there. I looked down again on that swarming mob and I must say my heart sank.

There had seemed to me to be a good deal of building up enthusiasm over Cornelia's appearance among her friends and professional people, who understand and appreciate the job she does. But for these boys she might just as well come out, I thought, and do a Chinese sing-song, classical play for all it would get to them. Friends and family, I maintain, always suffer as acutely as the performer, and I began to feel little ripples of chill and nausea, and a cold, unpleasant sweat on the forehead. I had had it before. I always have it when any friend of mine is about to do a professional job in public. It is therefore a little tiresome to me to hear the performers themselves describing their attacks of stage fright. I and their other friends have had just as acute symptoms.

A girl came out on the platform. I had seen her as we were pushing our way toward the front of the house and noticed that she was not in an apron or any uniform. One of the cute local young girls, I thought, who had volunteered to come in and dance for the boys. As I had squeezed past her I had heard her say to a soldier beside her, "I wish some of you military men would show me something real military." Her voice was low, and slowed down to a drawl by the weight of her southern accent. The volunteer master of ceremonies didn't give her name.

He simply said, "Here's someone who has some songs for you," and went across with her to the microphone. She stood grinning out at them in a friendly way, with a professional assurance, and yet young and shy, too. She turned the microphone back and forth a little to adjust it, gave a nod to the boy at the piano, and let the boys have *That Old Black Magic*. It was Dinah Shore. And after the yelling and stamping had died down with recognition of her after the first two words, she had to begin again.

My illness took a decided turn for the worse. This was the kind of thing those boys wanted. They would walk out on Cornelia probably or, worse, drown her out with hoots and catcalls. She was not their dish and she ought to know it. Better if we just slipped out again the back way. But there was no such luck. Dinah finished, and in spite of the roaring demands for more, was led off the stage by the master of ceremonies, who came back at once with Cornelia. He told the boys who she was, and there was a little applause.

"This," Cornelia said into the microphone, "is *Times Square*."

Times Square is one of her monologues which includes a swift change of characterization representing the types crossing the street in New York at Times Square. I thought again miserably she might as well have come out and done something in Chinese. They wouldn't know

Times Square. Her first character wasn't Chinese, but it was Italian—the Italian of a woman carrying a baby with two or three little ones hanging at her skirt, and she selling chewing gum. And there were, down in the front of the audience, some Italian-Americans, who, at the first word of what, Cornelia said afterward, was distinctly not "refined" Italian, broke into a bellow of surprise and pleasure. A girl with a gob who wanted to take her rowing in Central Park "slayed" the rest of them. (The audience was Army.) And quite a tragic characterization of a woman and her husband going for the last time to the opera before the husband left for Colorado where the wife said the climate would, of course, cure him in no time at all—brought on a bombardment of yells and roars and derisive noises. It turned out that a large group of the boys had just come into Los Angeles after some six or eight weeks in Colorado, and what they thought of the climate could be guessed in no time at all. I never saw anyone leave a state as rapidly as Cornelia got out of Colorado. She leapt over a good page and a half of lines and was into another characterization long before a traffic light could have changed at Times Square. But the audience was hers. It may not have been educated, but it understood people, especially Cornelia's people, and was crazy for them.

I asked, as soon as we left, to be taken somewhere for a little nourishment and a glass of beer. I had, I said, not been at all well. They were all very sympathetic, especially Cornelia. "Weren't you scared?" I finally asked her. "That was an awfully tough crowd and a mighty 'ornery' spot, just after Dinah Shore."

"No," she said, surprised, apparently, that I should ask. She had not even thought about it. The boys always went for *Times Square*—it was an awfully dependable piece.

It was, of course, unreasonable of me to be cross at *her*, but I was still not feeling at all well.

I went along to a command performance a few nights later. I didn't care whether her audience this time liked it or not. That is, I should be sorry, of course, but not visited with the symptoms of discomfort which I had had at the Canteen. Because, although this audience would be hundreds of times bigger, I would not see any of it. I was wrong about that. There is a small audience admitted, about a hundred and fifty men I should imagine; and it is made up entirely of men in the service. But the bulk of the audience is, of course, all over the world. And the command performance is given into a microphone, from which recordings are made and shipped wherever men are fighting. Dinah Shore was there that night, too. The man who runs these command performances said that she is one of the most tireless volunteers they have. Furthermore, that she did not wait to be asked. She would come around and offer to do some songs if they wanted her —and they always wanted her. Everybody else, he told

187

us, said the same thing about her. As a war worker on the job and begging for more, she couldn't be topped.

When she came off the stage after her songs, Cornelia started to tell her not only how much she liked to hear her sing, but loved to watch the way she used her hands. Dinah interrupted, and begged her not to say anything like that. It would make her self-conscious. "If I got to thinkin'," she said, "that I moved my hands around I'd be so interested in seein' what were they doin' I'd never open my mouth at all. I don't really know how to sing, either," she also told us. "But the only thing I can do is just not think about it."

The remaining numbers on the program that night were more difficult to procure, the head of the program said, than the most temperamental soloist. They were the request music. The requests were from members of that audience scattered all over the world, and they taxed the ingenuity of the oldest experts in sound effects: the music of a locomotive whistle in the valley when it was going to rain; birds, of course; and farm animals; not to mention the sound of milk from the cow to the pail. The one who asked for that wrote back saying that it was the most vivid thing he had ever heard—he could just see the old cow standing there being milked, and the milk splashing down into the pail. It is just as well that he was not there to see that the milk was water, and that a man standing on a chair poured it from a pitcher at that height through a funnel into a simple homely container on the floor—a container not often brought into such a conspicuous position from under the bed. Its public appearance on the program was not prompted either by a sense of coarse fun, nor a slip-shod use of whatever was handy. It was the final inspiration after every other conceivable type of receptacle had been tried and found wanting in sound.

Again, Cornelia's performance was a roaring success with her visible audience. I have not seen her at other performances like these, but I know that she gives them continuously all over the country, and I pay the deepest respect to this war work of hers.

Two days after the command performance, she did another bit of volunteer service. She was hurrying across one of busiest intersections in Hollywood when she saw a child ahead of her in great danger of being run down. The little boy was about five or six, she thought, dressed in appallingly bad taste in long pants and a Fedora hat. Some wretched little movie child actor, evidently, gotten up that way by an ambitious and misguided mother. He was ambling along as children seem always to elect to do at dangerous street crossings, sublimely unaware of a car which had swooped around the corner and was bearing down on him. Cornelia yelled, "Look where you're going, little boy," and leapt forward, snatching him up under the arms and jumping with him out of the path of the car. She carried him all the way to the opposite curb as an extra precaution of safety, and then set her little charge carefully upon the pavement. He squirmed around and presented the face of the angriest little midget of about fifty, which in her somewhat narrow acquaintanceship she had ever seen. He had on his lapel the large button photograph which identified him as a war worker. Evidently, she realized later, one of the little people—and she had read about them—employed in airplane factories to work on parts of a ship which could not be reached by persons of normal size. He was an important figure in war production, and he was fighting mad that an indignity should have occurred to him, and so unexpectedly. He swore roundly at Cornelia, twisting up his old man's face. It affected her zeal for service.

Chapter Twelve

The scenario was nearing an end. We had found a way, at last, out of the maze at Hampton Court; we took the girls to France, whipped them through a house of questionable repute at Rouen, hoping their stay would be too brief to attract the notice of Will Hays' office, brought them on to Paris—the last lap of the scenario, and of our stay in Hollywood. One week more would end them both. I think the week before the beginning and the end of a trip is always trying. You are anxious to go, and reluctant to leave, aware of all the things you meant to do and haven't got around to, obstinately determined to repeat within the week all the things you have enjoyed doing, in case you might not have another chance at them—and likely to be nervously irritable all round, the same feeling that I always have, condensed, when I have given my order irrevocably to a waiter.

We felt quite happy about the scenario, however, and about Mr. Hays' office, too. The happiness about Mr. Hays was due not only to our own achievement of virtue and refinement triumphant, but to our having met Mr. and Mrs. Hays. The meeting with them was in our hotel.

Cornelia pointed him out in the dining room. "That's Mr. Will Hays," she whispered, "greatest power in the whole motion picture business." Which I knew. "He doesn't know me," she went on, "but I was on a program once with him." At that moment Mr. Hays got up from his table and walked toward us.

Cornelia rose as he came nearer and put out her hand, saying she didn't suppose he remembered her, but she was Cornelia Otis Skinner. "Certainly, I know you," he told her, "you might as well ask if I remember the Washington Monument." Cornelia observed later she thought he might have chosen a happier association in memory than that implacable shaft of granite. Nevertheless she was pleased, and talked to him happily a minute or two when he said, "I'm interested in Emily. I think I know something about her, but I should like to find out where she is now." Cornelia pointed to me at the table approximately two feet away and Mr. Hays, acknowledging the introduction, called out across the room, "Jessie, bring our dessert over. Emily's here." Mrs. Hays got up immediately and started toward us. Mr. Hays went to meet her and relieve her of his plate of dessert and napkin, waving aside the waiters who sprang up around him. It gave Cornelia time to lean across and whisper to me that we might hear some of the inner workings of the whole industry. He was, of course, the very tops, she reiterated.

Mr. Hays was back at the table then with Mrs. Hays, whom he introduced, and they both apologized for breaking in on us. It was difficult to find phrases adequate to inform them how little they were breaking in, and how highly pleased we were at their coming. Mr. Hays was not one to waste time.

"Now then, Emily," he said, "if you came from Muncie, Indiana, what relation were C. M. Kimbrough and Lloyd?"

My grandfather, I told him, and my uncle.

"Well, then," he said, "your father must have been the oldest of the Kimbrough boys, the one that moved to Chicago." He turned to Mrs. Hays, "That was Hal, Jessie."

Mrs. Hays, he explained, was a Crawfordsville girl; he himself came from Sullivan.

I do not think I responded to them because he talked affectionately about my grandfather whom I idolized, and who, he said, had helped the young Will Hays. I am sure it was the quality in both of them of simplicity and homeliness to which I am bound in affection more than to any other qualities in the world. Mrs. Hays had read our book aloud to her mother and they had both liked it. That was endearing, too, but Mrs. Hays' own detailed, tender description of her mother, and of Crawfordsville, their Christmases there, and the family—(so that we might all know one another)—was heart warming. Perhaps that is a characteristic of some of the people in other states.

I can only assert that it is a characteristic of most of the people from the state of Indiana, and that I like it. But I could have told Cornelia, too, that another characteristic of people from Indiana is that they talk about Indiana and the people from it. I knew that neither Cornelia nor I would hear talk of the movies—not from the moment that towns in Indiana were mentioned. It promised to be an old Hoosier get-together, and it was. We were all kin.

Jessie, Mr. Hays said, had even been in a house just like the one we were in in Rouen—by mistake, too, he and Mrs. Hays both interrupted quickly. She'd been traveling abroad with a group of girls and a chaperon, and hadn't even known the kind of place it was until long afterwards. But there was no doubt in the world that that was what it was, so she could understand perfectly how it could have happened to us. Mr. Hays could understand it, too. People kidded him sometimes, and said that he thought that if anything came from Indiana it was all right. That wasn't true, of course. Still, he'd be inclined to think that what we girls did wouldn't be anything he could object to. Cornelia observed in the elevator that personally she could find more lively accounts in the *National Geographic* than our evening of life among the Hoosiers, but that this farewell of Mr. Hays was compensation.

The promise had sustained us throughout the scenario. If things looked dubious, our slogan of courage was "Mr.

Hays said it would be all right." As a matter of fact, we thought it was all right, too—simple, wholesome fare, with maybe just a dash of maraschino.

We had stopped going over after lunch to watch any scenes being made. We had become a little tired of it all. Now that I realized I was not going to see them any more, I regretted not having gone every day and was irritated at having become blasé. In the last week there was no time. But we did knock off work every afternoon to go across the street from the Paramount entrance to the little sweet shop where the studio people gathered. Why those places are called sweet shops I cannot imagine, and they are all alike. There is one in every village. It is the center, too, of any boarding school or college extra-curricular life, and it is always dirty, musty, dark and crowded. It sells candy, magazines, and dusty, fly-specked toys, cigars and cigarettes; it has a soda fountain, and booths with high-backed wooden benches along the wall. This one sold liquor, too, and we sometimes took home a bottle if we were having people for cocktails or dinner. But I never saw anyone in the booths having a drink, only cokes or chocolate soda. Charlie Brackett had tea. The talk was steady, sometimes loud, always sharp, always shop. The air was so thick with smoke that everyone's words were muffled. At a little after six, the telephone would begin ringing—Mr. Brackett's office to say that the rushes were ready to be shown—and Mr. Brackett would leave on a

195

run. Little by little the crowd would thin out, called to their rushes, or dinner, maybe. But in the evening, the proprietor said, he got a fresh crowd, people staying late or coming back to work. It was a repulsive little place, and I miss it very much.

Then we tried to catch up on the after-work places we'd missed. Ever since our arrival we had heard of the Turn-About Theatre, and so we went there determinedly one night of the last week. It was amusing, but an oil well pumping busily in the middle of the boulevard on the way to the theatre was more memorable. It was a very busy boulevard, too, but the oil well, I was told, had been there for years, and as long as it operated twenty-four hours a day it could not be removed. So the boulevard had been built around it.

It was like drinking the vin du pays to see such sights as this, and they were memories that I wanted to carry back with me. So we drove again one day down the famous Wilshire Boulevard where, within a few blocks, we could read, with pleasure, announcements of the "Page Boy Maternity Shop"; the candy establishment entitled, "Awful Fresh MacFarland"; the billboard with luminous lettering which said "Get the Church-Going Habit." This was illustrated by the picture of a little girl with long golden curls and a crisp white party dress, standing on tip-toe to light the candles on an altar. Across the way another hope for eternity read on a billboard, "Complete

196

Funerals and Lasting Care, As Low as $66, by Utter Mc-
Kinley." This explained, too, the current phrase at the
studio that anything to an extra degree was an "Utter
McKinley." I always hoped, too, driving down the boulevard, that I might see again one day the lady in slacks
and mink coat who carried a lace parasol, but I only saw
her once.

Side by side with the memorable signs were some of the
smartest and most luxurious shops in this country. I have
seen women in them dressed with as great chic, too, as
I have seen anywhere, including Paris. But I also saw
a woman trying on a sumptuous silver fox cape, reaching
almost to the ground, who revealed—when she exchanged
the silver fox for a sable—a shopping costume underneath
of a cotton romper suit, bare legs, and sneakers.

I went a last time to the Farmers' Market, alone, because Cornelia is a more passive food consumer than I,
taking it pretty much as it comes. I like to start as near
the source as possible and enjoy it every step of the way.
Norman Brock had been the one, of course, to show me
this delectable place. We had bought the food there for
our Marian Anderson party—he and another Philadelphian
up for the week-end from a nearby camp and I. "Baby
Bunches" was the unhappy name of our favorite stall,
where we had bought avocados no larger than a fore-
finger, carrots the size of a thumb nail, beets just as small,
and artichokes a baby could have held in his hand. And

then we had stood in line at the lunch counter called "Fish and Chips" to wait our turn for paper plates piled high with scalding hot fried shrimps and the cold tomato catsup sauce to dip them in. We could have had an equally high mound of cracked crabmeat, and it was hard to choose between. But there was not a hot dog nor a hamburger stand to be seen.

I took the shrimps again when I came back alone for a last gorge, playing a childish, superstitious game with myself that if I took the cracked crab I should have had everything, and there would be no need to come back. But something left untried might bring me that way again.

Cornelia did not accompany me, either, when I went to lunch with my great Aunt Wilmina who lives in Wilmington, Ohio, but was spending the winter in Los Angeles. And she missed a treat, because Aunt Wilmina is an inveterate sight-seer. She took me to lunch at the Bullock's Wilshire store and to make the tour of its windows and spring display, because, she said, I had been working so hard I had not had a chance to get around to see anything. She was sorry—in fact, she was highly annoyed—that the sight-seeing busses were not running because she preferred them to taxis or trolleys—the conversation of the guide made the ride more interesting. She had, she explained, bought a car out here, and she kept it in Los Angeles and brought along a nice boy from Wilmington to drive it. But it made her nervous in the city so she used it only for trips. If the Chamber of Commerce were going to act up this way about the sight-seeing busses, she wasn't at all sure she would even come back another winter.

That night I went to dinner at Mike Romanoff's, another farewell visit. As long as Aunt Wilmina is on the war-path I wish she could turn her hand to him. I find his hauteur not so endearing to me as it seems to be to others. But I never saw his place when it wasn't packed, and people turned away—unless they were important.

Dave Chasen, on the other hand, I like almost as much as Mr. Behrman, but I should have gone to his restaurant once more even without him or his food, to look again with delight at the décor of the tiny foyer—the portrait done with classic restraint, superb brush work, and beautiful subtlety of treatment, of W. C. Fields as Queen Victoria. The food is, also, I think, the best in Hollywood. There is, or was then, Eastern beef for Norman Brock and sand dabs for me, that Pacific Coast delicacy for which I would forego almost any amount of Eastern animals.

The Walter Abels gave a tea on our last Sunday, and we drove out to Beverly Hills where we had gone so often to the Charlie Bracketts'. I do not know whether they emerge on week days or not, but on Saturdays and Sundays there are always sprinkled along the road, crones and trolls who hold up, like a bridge hand, a spread-out array of booklets. And across their chests they carry large placards which say, "Maps to the Stars." But they are not maps for astronomers nor for the casting of horoscopes. They are directions to the houses of the Hollywood stars so that the tourist may trace his gaping route from one famous dwelling to another. In these days, however, of restricted travel, the roadside standers are not entirely confident in their trade; so they have developed a side-line. In the other hand they hold up for sale boxes of crackerjack.

We were late because Cornelia had given her monologue of *The Minute Man* on the Charlie McCarthy program, and when we got to the Abels, Jimmy Cagney, they told us, had just left, which was a great disappointment to me. I admire him as an actor, and his was, I thought, by far the best speech at the Academy dinner—forthright, unaffected, and brief. It seemed to me quite in character, too, that the reason he had left the tea, along with Walter Abel, was that they were concerned over a problem of motion picture extras and had gone to a meeting about it.

We came home by way of the Charlie Bracketts'. They live only ten or fifteen minutes farther on, and it seemed to both of us very unintelligent to be within possible reach, and not see them.

When I was taken visiting as a child I used, they tell me, to assemble before the front door a mound of all the things to which I had taken a fancy, and at the moment of departure would announce confidently that I

200

guessed I would take these home with me. I think it a great pity that as I grew older I gave up that practice. I should certainly have liked to assemble and bring home with me Mr. Behrman, Morrie Ryskind, whom I saw, alas, only one night at a dinner, Dave Chasen, and the Charlie Bracketts, together with some sand dabs, cracked crab, and baby artichokes.

We packed the next day. I seemed, as a matter of fact, to have accumulated quite a mound. In the process of fitting it in, I stood with one foot on the lid of my trunk, the distance between the lid and the lock giving me the stance of a ballet dancer at the practice rail, and at that moment Cornelia telephoned. Could I, she asked, come downstairs right away? Her tone was ominous. I left the trunk, hoping, as she says in one of her monologues, that the things in it would just settle somehow, and hurried down the stairs.

I knocked on the door and she said, "It's open." Something about her tone—a sort of Lady Macbeth timbre, gave me a sense of foreboding. Her voice sounded near the door, too. It seemed odd that she didn't open it herself. But I pushed it. She was standing just inside, and she was holding in front of her the white satin Valentine heart.

I had not thought of it since the day of our arrival. Neither, mercifully, had she, she said. She had hidden it in one of the eight or nine closets her apartment provided.

But she had found it again, by opening every door to make sure nothing was left behind. And, she emphasized bitterly, she was *not* going to leave that for the management to discover, but she was certainly not going to take it with her. I would have to think of something. I may say that taxed me. We had even lost the cardboard box into which we had folded it on our arrival. We were, moreover, entertaining a secret (not admitted to each other) hope that there might be two or three people to see us off. We both knew, too, that *I* would not carry it again.

In the end it was Cornelia who had the solution. We would, she said, give it to Bob Hope. He had promised us an autographed picture for each of our children. We had, in turn, promised him a copy of our book. He had not sent us the picture; therefore we would, to remind him, send the book, and we would send it on the satin heart.

We carried it to the studio the next morning and we were on foot the last fifteen minutes or so, because we turned in our car on the way. But nobody noticed us, or our burden. In the office we penned a letter, reminding him of the photograph and telling him, unnecessarily, that we were sending with our book a souvenir of our respect and admiration for his work. Then we called a messenger, explained to her that the book was to be carried in upon the heart like a cocktail on a tray, and the letter, rolled up

202

like a scroll, placed beside it. After that we sat back to wait.

The report was not long in coming. Lyle Rooks, our friend, brought it. We need not, she said, have worried about the messenger's delivery of our offering. She was, after all, a Hollywood messenger, and so, at the entrance to the studio where Bob, with a company of about a hundred and fifty was working on a sequence in *Let's Face It*, she had adjusted the book and the scroll on the pillow, and advanced toward the stage. She did not, however, come like a maid carrying a cocktail on a tray, but like a page boy in grand opera bearing a crown and sceptre on a pillow, four beats to each step, and each step knee high. No camera man nor director, not even Bob Hope's hoarse entreaty could swerve her. Straight as a carrier pigeon and as unfaltering, she came, and when she reached him, dropped to her knees and extended the offering.

"Were they angry?" we asked fearfully. Well, not exactly, Lyle admitted, at least they were not acting that way. They were at the moment sending to the publicity department for photographers and copy writers. They were going to have the messenger re-do the whole thing and take pictures of it to release to the papers. It was a good gag.

We said good-bye regretfully to Jim at the gymnasium. I could have added him to my mound of what to bring home with me. He has never been to New York, he had told us. But as we left, he called out that if the picture had a New York opening, by God, he would come on for it, and, what was more, as the picture started, he'd jump on the stage from somewhere and he'd yell, "Skinny and Emily, the Japs are coming." He might even bring along a piece of a Venetian blind to rattle. What a laugh that would be. Would *he* ever get a laugh out of that? We promised him to get a laugh this time, too, if he would do it, and I have no reason to suppose he would not.

We visited all the sets again with Lyle, to whom we had become devoted. There was one, she said, she would hate for us to miss. We were glad we were to have the opportunity to see it, whatever it was, because Lyle is not given to enthusiasms. It turned out to be the scene in which two heralds on either side of a doorway advance in time to music to the center of the stage, raise their trumpets, pretend to blow, turn, and march back again. Well, we had not seen it for three weeks and there was a new herald. We could see no other changes.

When we came back up to our office, Eleanor, our secretary, was waiting. We had come to love her in the last ten days—ever since we'd found we had her. She held out presents for us—yellow copy paper which we had admired, and two boxes for each of us of the soft pencils which the office provided, and which we had found superior to any we had ever gripped. I do not know how she

came by this gift, and I should not have dreamed of inquiring. We only thanked her with all our hearts. But I
wonder, uneasily, if Mr. Y. Frank Freeman knows that I
am at this moment using one which may not have been
accounted for in his budget.

We didn't stop at Sheridan's office to say good-bye to
Rose. We would come in the morning on our way to the
train, when Sheridan and his wife were going to drive us
to the station. But we did pause at the little booth on the
sidewalk to collect our last salary check, a separate check
for each of us, with the paymaster's grin.

That night we went to see Nina to tell her good-bye.
Margo was to have come, but could not get away from
work of some kind at the studio. Garry, too, was out drawing pictures to get into the Army. But Zoia was there and
the three of us let the dogs in and out, while Nina talked
about the Russian party she had given, which had been
wonderful—everybody would tell us that. And it was very
disagreeable of us not to have come. (It had been the
same night as the Academy dinner.) And the work of her
pupils—those who were not womiting. And the balcony
of her cottage at Laguna which had fallen down.

We said we must go—it was midnight—and it was then
that Nina thought of her autobiography. She was trying
to write it in English. There was so much she wanted to
say, and no one else could say it for her. God had sent
us to help her. We would know what things were impor-

tant and what should be cut out. She would read us what she had written, and we would be truthful. It would be artists talking to artist. She thundered up the stairs like a platoon, and down again with a child's copybook. Messages floated out of it on scraps of paper all the way downstairs, and when we had salvaged and she had arranged them, they turned out to be the first two chapters. She read them while we stood at the front door.

After I had put up my window that night, I stood for a long time looking across the face of the soft hills where a supercolossal sign read, "Hollywoodland." We had thought it symbolic, perhaps, that a Hollywood view should be labeled, but were told that that was not half as self-consciously symbolic as the suicide of an unsuccessful young actress who, after writing a letter to the papers to explain the symbolism, had ended her life by jumping off the top of one of the letters of the sign. Since our arrival the letter "H" had unaccountably begun to droop. Now in the moonlight it read, with a sort of sad, Cockney gaiety, "ollywoodland." Perhaps the whole of Hollywoodland was as cock-eyed as the sign, and a little bit Cockney, too. That was what its publicity would have you believe. I hadn't found it to be like that. But then, I had liked it, which of course always colors one's judgment. I had not been prepared to like it either. I had come in a critical frame of mind as I always am, I think, when I do not feel entirely sure of myself. I had certainly felt far from sure of myself about doing a job in Hollywood, and I could not remember ever having enjoyed a job more.

I should like, I decided, looking across to where the "H" had been, to come back again, if I could, to do another job of work, and I had worked hard. If this were the land of lotuses they had not been part of my diet. Still, I should like to come back for the food, too; and I went to bed.

We left with Al, the clerk at the desk (short for Alamo), packages to be sent on of what we had been unable to get into our bags. Even so we could not get our accumulated luggage and ourselves into one taxi. So we hired another and with the friends who had joined us to see us off, made quite a procession to Sheridan's office where we were to stop for him. I had, too, lost the key of my trunk so many times that I was threatening to carry it the rest of the way home between my teeth, and was, perhaps, a little edgy. I said anxiously that I did hope Sheridan wouldn't hold us up, with all the taxis and people downstairs, and so much to do at the station. We said good-bye to Rose in the outer office and opened Sheridan's door beyond. He was ready to go, but as he got up from his desk, Cornelia, taking on a dreamy look, drifted over to her accustomed chair and sat down. "I've been thinking," she said, and began pulling off her gloves, finger by finger, "that in that scene at the college dance we ought to have the vamp do successfully all the things she had been trying to teach Cornelia to do and have her get Cornelia's beau by the very same lines Cornelia couldn't pull off."

I do not know how long it was before anyone spoke and then it was Sheridan. "Come in, Rose," he said, "we're going to do the first scene."

Chapter Thirteen

Two weeks ago I received in the mail what is called the shooting script of our picture. That, it had been explained to me, was the process of breaking down the scenario into camera shots and technical arrangements. It had, they had assured us, nothing to do with the scenario writing itself.

If that is so, then certainly the camera shots and the lighting do extraordinary things. Out of the entire piece there are left only here and there, like the fragments after an air raid, an occasional phrase or sentence of ours. And yet, the spirit of our book is there, and the comedy it irks me to admit, is perhaps, funnier. Sometimes there is the echo of one of our scenes, as we wrote it in Sheridan's office, but it is far away and indistinct. An indignant letter, attached, from the Hays' office refuses to pass any part of the Rouen scene, and there was no communication whatever from Mr. Hays himself.

However, a week ago Hollywood was on the telephone. Paramount was calling. Would Miss Kimbrough, Paramount said, like to come back to Hollywood for two months, while the picture was made, to act as a technical adviser?

There is nothing Miss Kimbrough would like better to do.

Her ticket is bought; her trunk has gone. And when the last word here is written, she'll be on her way on the Super Chief—to Hollywood—from where she will telephone her twins every Sunday morning.

Haverford, Pennsylvania
July 15, 1943

WOULD MISS KIMBROUGH, PARAMOUNT SAID, LIKE TO COME BACK TO HOLLYWOOD FOR TWO MONTHS?